TIME MANAGEMENT IN THE LIFE OF A SCHOLAR

Adonis & Abbey Publishers Ltd
St James House
13 Kensington Square,
London, W8 5HD
United Kingdom

Website: http://www.adonis-abbey.com
E-mail Address: editor@adonis-abbey.com

Nigeria:
Suites C4 & C5 J-Plus Plaza
Asokoro, Abuja, Nigeria
Tel: +234 (0) 7058078841/08052035034

British Library Cataloguing-in-Publication Data
A catalogue record for this book is available from the British Library

ISBN: 978-1-909112-53-7

TIME MANAGEMENT IN THE LIFE OF A SCHOLAR

Kabiru Isa Dandago

ADONIS & ABBEY
PUBLISHERS LTD

TABLE OF CONTENTS

PREFACE

Time management is a subject that concerns every individual and every organisation. Individuals have God - endowed time to spend in achieving their objectives in life; organisations are formed by individuals or employ individuals whose time they buy/employ for the achievement of their set objectives and goals. Individuals and organisations have to show concern about effective and efficient time management.

At the individual level, it is clear that too many needs (not to talk of wants) are there for the limited time available. Depending on what a person does for a living or the level of personal development at which a person is in his/her life, appropriate skills and behaviors have to be acquired or adopted for effective and efficient time management. This is necessary for the achievement of short-term and long-term objectives. It is, therefore, a general challenge for persons in the public or private sectors to master the art and science of time management.

For a person in the educational sector of any economy of the world, especially the scholar, the challenge of 'time' is two-fold: making its effective management as part of his/her life and promoting its management as a subject of study. This book aims to guide the scholar as to how to make effective and efficient utilisation of his/her time for high level of productivity and to encourage the scholar, especially management scientist, to pursue research works and other academic activities in the area of time management so as to promote it as a field of study.

This book consists of eleven chapters, with Chapter One being an introduction. Chapter Two reviews available and accessible English-language-based-literature on time and its management. The fact, from the literature, is that there is no universally acceptable definition of time, time management and other related terminologies; and that there is no universally acceptable model or theory of time management. This means that a lot needs to be done to make time management occupy its rightful position in the management science literature. One way of demonstrating commitment to that effect is the publication of this book by Adonis & Abbey Publishers Limited.

Chapter Three conceptualises who a scholar is, emphasising on the need for the scholar to show high level commitment as a researcher, teacher, and community servant who takes learning as his/her lifestyle. Chapter Four contextualises time management as per the perception of this book, addressing the concept of time and time management, and discussing how a scholar could be accepted as a time planner, organiser, director, controller and decision maker.

Chapter Five addresses the issue of time scarcity, starting with the basic cause of it to all time users, and then argues for five other causes. Chapter Six is about time audit and why it is necessary for effective utilisation of time. Chapter Seven is about time stealers that affect the scholar, illustrating just five notorious stealers. Chapter Eight is on how scholars generally waste their time as they adopt some bad behaviors that are against effective time management.

Chapter Nine reviews Stephen R. Covey's time management grid/matrix to show how a scholar could make excellent use of it to ensure efficiency and effectiveness in his/her time utilisation. Chapter Ten highlights and discusses twenty golden guides/rules for the excellent time management practice expected of a scholar. Chapter Eleven recapitulates the first ten chapters and highlights research potentials exposed by each of the first ten chapters of the book.

This book challenges all scholars at all levels of the educational sector to be role models on the art and science of time management. These scholars could be at the primary/basic school level, secondary/high school level, tertiary educational institutions (universities, polytechnics, colleges of education, etc), research institutes/centers, or at the informal educational institutions. It is also a challenge for them to go deep into research on various aspects of time management so as to establish acceptable principles, models and theories, and then test their practices.

The book also appeal to educational institutions (especially management-based) and relevant professional institutes/bodies to sponsor researches, publications(like journals and newsletters), seminars, conferences, and even conventions on various aspects of time management so as to promote it as a field of study.

Although the book has the scholar in mind, other users of time in the various sectors of an economy, and at various levels, should adapt and adopt the guides given in Chapters 4-10 for ensuring effective and efficient management and utilisation of their time.

Prof. Dr. Kabiru Isa Dandago, FCA, FNIM, MNES, ACTI, AAIF
The Author: *kidandago@gmail.com*

ACKNOWLEDGEMENTS

First and foremost, the author expresses gratitude to Almighty Allah for the thoughts and actions culminating into the write up of the book. I pray for Allah to make the book a big blessing to humanity in various positive ways as it is put to use by scholars and other users of time in various sectors of different economies of the world.

I would want to express my sincere gratitude to the authorities of the Universiti Utara Malaysia (UUM), under the visionary leadership of Prof. Dato' Wira Dr. Mohamed Mustafa Ishak, for the opportunity given to me to spend my one year sabbatical leave and another year of leave of absence in the School of Accountancy (SOA), College of Business (COB). It was in this School that I presented a public lecture on time management after which I was required to write a book on the subject matter. I owe a special gratitude to Puan Rosma Ishak of the UUM Press, who encouraged/challenged me to embark on the project of converting the PowerPoint presentation slides into a book for the benefit of many interested scholars and other time users who could not attend the public lecture. She feels such a book would be a big contribution to time management literature from UUM. Puan Rosma, I am very grateful for this challenge and for your continuous reminders, through emails, for the draft manuscript to be made available so that the book could see the light of the day.

I owe a great deal of appreciation for my colleagues in the SOA-UUM and numerous post graduate students who attended the public lecture and made useful contributions on many more issues that should have been covered in the presentation, which have now been taken care of in this book. I accord special regards and respects to the Dean of SOA, Prof. Dr. Kamil MD Idris, the Deputy Dean, Assoc. Prof. Dr. Zuaini Bt Ishak, the Chief Operating Officer (COO) of SOA, Puan Maimuna Mohamed (who was a participant at the public lecture), the two HODs (Dr Shamharir and Dr Basariah), and all the other academic and administrative staff of SOA-UUM. They have been always ready to guide, assist and encourage me on the ways to ensure that I live up to the requirements of my KPI.

I extend a lot of thanks to the authorities of Bayero University, Kano-Nigeria, under the dynamic leadership of Professor Abubakar Adamu Rasheed, *mni*, MFR, for my release to go to UUM as a Visiting Professor for two years, and for the ever continuous encouragement for me to promote scholarship in that university and beyond. I am sure the

Vice Chancellor, being an excellent time manager, would be very happy with the "birth" of this book.

I thank my family members (four of whom were at the historic SOA-UUM time management lecture, as observers) for their patience, understanding and support throughout the period of my sojourns at UUM and for their encouraging comments on the write up of this book. Barrister Binta (my wife), Salman, Usama and Asiya played observatory role during the 8th January, 2014 public lecture, while Khalid, Sumayya, UmmulSalma, Nasiba and Musa were in Nigeria at that time.

Lastly, but not the least, I would like to thank each and everyone who have in no small measure contributed to the successful completion of this book, including those reviewers who provided useful editorial comments and language editing.

Prof. Dr. Kabiru Isa Dandago, FCA, FNIM, MNES, ACTI, AAIF
The Author: *kidandago@gmail.com*

DEDICATION

To Whom: This book is dedicated to the memory of **His Royal Highness (HRH), the immediate past Emir of Kano, Alhaji (Dr) Ado Abdullahi Bayero, CFR, LLD, JP.** He passed away on 6th June, 2014, when the book write up was about to be completed.

His Time Management credentials: He was an epitome of time management throughout the 51 years of his reign as Emir of Kano, Kano State, Nigeria. He was highly respected for his commitment to time keeping, punctuality, zero tolerance to time wasters, delegation of responsibilities for time saving and high degree of priority setting. One of the greatest lessons he taught his subjects is about how they could be excellent time managers in whatever they do in their lives.

His Birth Day: Friday, 25th July, 1930
His Day of Ascension to Throne: Wednesday, 23rd October, 1963
His Demise Day: Friday, 6th June, 2014
May his gentle soul rest in perfect peace!

Late HRH Alhaji (Dr) Ado Bayero, CFR, LLD, JP

ABOUT THE AUTHOR

Professor Dr. Kabiru Isa Dandago has been a Visiting Professor of Accounting at the Universiti Utara Malaysia (UUM), for the period August 2012 to August 2014. He served as Chair, Bayero University Consultancy Services Unit (July 2008 to July 2012); as Dean, Faculty of Social and Management Sciences, Bayero University (June 2004-June 2008) and as Head, Department of Accounting of the same University (April 2002- April 2006).

Prof. Kabiru joined the services of Bayero University, Nigeria in September 1990 and rose to the rank of Professor of Accounting in October 2007. He also occupies the professorial chair on Taxation endowed by the Federal Inland Revenue Service (FIRS), at the Kogi State University, Nigeria.

Prof. Kabiru has attended over 50 conferences, nationally and internationally. He has authored, co-authored and edited 25 books in the areas of Accounting, Finance, Management and Economics. He has published 65 researched articles in national and international peer-reviewed journals and books of readings. He has visited 20 countries of the world, mainly for academic and professional conferences and interactions.

Prof. Kabiru holds B. Sc, M. Sc (Accounting), MBA, PhD (Economics) degrees. He is a Fellow of the Institute of Chartered Accountants of Nigeria (ICAN), Fellow of the Nigerian Institute of Management (NIM), Fellow of the Nigerian Institute of Treasury Managers (NITM), Life Member of the Nigerian Economic Society (NES), Member, Chartered Institute of Taxation of Nigeria (CITN), Member, Institute of Management Consultants (IMC), Member, Business Ethics Network of Africa (BEN-Africa), and holder of Associate Award in Islamic Finance (AAIF) from IBFIM, Malaysia.

As a certified management professional and consultant, he has been organising training workshops and seminars for managers and supervisors of public and private sector organisations on the art of time management for enhanced productivity in the workplace. Since the introduction of the Master's degree programme on Treasury Management (MTM) at Bayero University, Nigeria in 2006, he has been the facilitator of the course titled: 'Time Management Process', until his departure to the Universiti Utara Malaysia (UUM) on sabbatical leave and leave of absence.

Over the 24 years of his working life in the University system, Prof. Kabiru has come to realise that most scholars in the system and those in other levels of the educational sector are not according time management the attentions it deserves. These required attentions are: (i) in respect of its effective management to achieve desired results and (ii) in respect of promoting it as a subject of study at various levels. This book is an attempt at addressing these two issues.

CHAPTER ONE

INTRODUCTION

1.1 The Life of a Scholar

The life of a serious scholar is a life demanding almost the whole of the 24 hours in a day for discharging many academic, administrative and community responsibilities. It is a life that should not tolerate wasting a second of its time. This calls for the need for the art of time management and utilisation to be emphasised in the life of a scholar, since it is the key to his/her success in discharging various responsibilities.

To perform well as a scholar or professional, one has to show effectiveness in the management of the resources at his/her disposal, the most important of which is "time". Effective management of any resource (especially time) requires demonstration of good appreciation of management functions: planning, organising, directing and controlling.

A scholar has to always plan how to spend his/her time in the face of too many competing activities that demand his/her time. This calls for effective budgeting and budgetary control to be applied on the limited time available. The scholar has to be very organised as the limited time is used to accomplish many tasks, demonstrating principles of prioritisation, delegation and time consciousness.

A scholar has to ensure that direction is given as time is utilised to achieve set goals and objectives, and the 'control function' of ensuring that things are going according to plan should be brought to bear. Again, the scholar is expected to always make comparison, at appropriate intervals, between the planned time usage and the actual time utilisation, with a view to investigate the causes and implications of the variance that is bound to arise.

1.2 A Scholar and Effective Time Management

Effectiveness is about doing the right thing or the ability to bring about the intended result. For this reason, the term is frequently used in appreciation of sound management of resources (Heller, 1995). The resources to be effectively managed using the good culture of discipline, hard work, and sense of maturity are money, materials, machines, men and time. To manage all of these, there is the need for a high level of effectiveness to be demonstrated by the "manager".

There is always the need for effective time management at all levels, be it individual, family, organisational and/or government. This is because if time is not effectively managed, goals and objectives could not be achieved and, so, there is bound to be backwardness in the life of the individual, family, organisation or government. This would negatively affect the community or country as a whole, slowing down the process of growth and development. It could, therefore, be argued that poor time management is one of the main causes of the poverty and other forms of backwardness many individuals and nations suffer from in this world!

1.3 Equality in Time Endowment

Time, as a resource, is needed for all we do in life and so, no matter how well a person plans to use other resources, he/she must plan for the influence of time in achieving his/her objectives. Public and private sector organisations are also expected to appreciate this fact of life and plan well for the influence of time as they set to achieve various organisational objectives. In particular, organisations should value their employed time, vested in their staff, and make effective utilisation of that time for the achievement of the organisational goals and objectives.

Time is the only resource God endowed on people equality. The leaders of the G7 (wealthiest nations of the world) or those of the G20 (most developed nations of the world) could not claim to have more time than leaders of the poorest countries of the world (mainly in Africa, Asia and Latin America). The Chief Executive Officers (CEOs) of the leading multinational enterprises in the world could not claim to have more time than leaders of the ailing business organisations in the developing or backward economies of the world.

None of the leading billionaires in the world (like Bill Gates, Carlos Slim, Amancio Ortega, Warren Buffet, Larry Ellison, Charles Koch, Ted Turner, Richard Branson, Andrew Forrest, Hasso Plattner, Christopher Cooper-Hohn, David Sainsbury, Mo Ibrahim, Patrice Motsepe, Vincent Tan Chee Yioun, Azim Premji, Aliko Dangote, etc) would claim to have an hour more than the 24 hours endowed to them by God in a day, the 7 days in a week, the 4 weeks in a month, the 12 months in a year, the 10 years a decade or the 40 years in a generation. Just as they have these

16

dimensions of time in a limited sense, the poorest people of the world do not have less!

So, time, which is the most important asset to humanity, is equally endowed. Success in life (at the individual and organisational levels) is, therefore, greatly dependent on effective time management. A poor time manager cannot rely on luck to continue to record success in discharging responsibilities. The more you throw away your most important asset (time), the more failures you record in life and the more problems you face in your day-to-day activities.

Scholars at various levels of educational pursuits are greatly challenged by the nature of their responsibilities to show effective time management for them to achieve academic excellence and show the future generations of ways to excel in their chosen careers.

1.4 Related Issues Covered in Subsequent Chapters

Is time management well conceptualised, theoretised and adequately researched into as a part of the management science literature? Who is a scholar? What actually is time management? How should a scholar be effectively managing his/her time? Is there scarcity in time? How is time audit conducted, by whom and for whom? What are time wasters in the life of a scholar and other time users? What does time management matrix signify? What are the golden guides for excellent time management? These are the questions addressed in the subsequent chapters of this book.

But, let's appreciate the presence of time management in the management science literature. How far have scholars gone in establishing the presence of time management in the literature?

CHAPTER TWO

TIME MANAGEMENT IN THE LITERATURE

2.1 Is Time Management Really There?

Time, as a resource, requires a lot of attention from individuals, organisations and government (the three components of any economy). It deserves greater research attention than any of the other resources God endows on mankind. As stated in chapter 1, time is the only resource God endowed on human beings equally. Its management, therefore, requires the attention of the academia, the professionals, policy makers and implementers, businessmen and women, students or just everybody.

But, unfortunately, it appears as if time management is not enjoying the attention other resources, like money/finance, inventory, fixed assets/property, account receivables, etc, enjoy from users and researchers. There is a wealth of literature on each of the subjects of financial management or cash management, fixed asset management, facilities management, inventory management, account receivable management and even intellectual capital or intangible asset management. One also comes in contact with a wealth of literature on each of the subjects of marketing management, portfolio management, personnel or human resource management, banking risk management, conflict management, operations management, sports management, etc.

A search into the English-based literature would reveal that time management cannot compete with any of the issues raised above in terms of patronage from the academic and professional writers, and in terms of promotion of the subject matter as a discipline of study. You hardly find any university, college or school that teaches time management as a specific course of study in any programme or even as a general study course; not to talk of offering time management as a programme leading to an award of a degree or diploma. Time management topics are usually attachments to other courses of study; and that is if the institution concerned feels that time management should be given any attention at all at any level of study.

In this chapter, effort is made to 'comb up' some contributions made to the field of time management in the literature: appreciating the few efforts of some professionals, academics and religious scholars. A bibliographical list of relevant works to the subject of time management is provided at the end of this book. Scholars, who are expected to demonstrate effective time management, should take the apparent dearth of literature in this important area of study as another big challenge, apart from the challenge of serving as effective time managers. The challenge is, however, more posed to scholars in the field of management science (business management/administration, accounting, finance, entrepreneurship, etc) than to scholars in other fields of study. They are expected to popularise time management as an area of study whose time has come.

2.2 Works of Professional Time Management Speakers

Most of the write ups on time management are from public motivational speakers in the field of management science. These professional speakers, coaches and mentors in management science have delivered many public speeches, class lectures, seminars and workshops on time management. They have written many professional papers, essays, pamphlets and books on various aspects of time management, some of which are accessible on the websites dedicated to their professional and humanitarian works on the subject of time management. Some of the renowned time management experts, who use English as a medium of communication, are Stephen R Covey, Donald E. Wetmore, Wendy Hearn, Margaret Spencer Dixon, Janice Cuny, Dorathy Cudaback, etc.

Stephen R. Covey was one of the most influential and motivational speakers, teachers and writers in the field of time management that ever lived. His most popular book is: "The Seven Habits of Highly Effective People", which emphasises the need for effective time management for people to become effective in whatever they do in life. Habit 2 titled: "Begin with the End in Mind", dominates the contents of the book as issues raised therein were carried across the other habits 3-7, expected of highly effective people.

Habit 2 is illustrated with the popular time management quadrants analysis discussed in detail in chapter 9 of this book. Most effective people were described as those that prioritise Quadrants 1 and 2 activities and de-emphasise Quadrant 3 and 4 activities. These issues were the supporting subjects of discussion as the other Habits were discussed.

Covey's other popular books are centered on time management related issues for effective management of personal life. For his contributions to the field of time management, as a professional speaker and writer, the late Covey has enjoyed and is still enjoying a lot of accolades, respect and good prayers from businessmen and women, managers of private and public sector organisations, students of management at all levels, media practitioners and scholars.

Donald E. Wetmore is another highly respected professional speaker and writer on time management, who had done a lot of studies and published many professional essays in the field of time management. In his more than 30 years experience on delivering time management speeches and conducting seminars and workshops to a wide variety of participants, Wetmore has released many Time Management Tips that are available on the website of the **Productivity Institute-Time Management Seminars**.

Some of the issues addressed by Wetmore in his essays are: Top Five Time Management Mistakes; Stop Wasting Time; Successful Time Management; How to Get Control of Your Time and Your Life; Top Best Time Management practices; Five Best Time Management Habits Executives should Practice; Time Management Secrets; Time Management Facts and Figures; The Time Thieves; Time Management Reality; Time Management Myth; Ten Time Savers; Five Best Time Management Do's for Students; Four Time Management Don'ts for Students; etc.

Wetmore sees the 5 Big Time Wasters as poor planning, procrastination, interruptions, failure to delegate, and attending meetings. He concluded his description of poor planning with what he calls "Six P's": Poor Planning Produces Pretty Poor Performance. This is in line with the conclusion reached by another time management expert, Alan Lakein, that "Failure to Plan is Planning to Fail".

Wendy Hearn is a coach, strategist, writer, entrepreneur, speaker and principal of Wendy Hearn Coaching, an international coaching company on time management and other personal performance enhancement issues. She works with business owners, leaders and executives who want strategies to be successful, move to excellence and achieve profound breakthroughs. She is passionate, inspiring, and enthusiastic. She is blessed with contagious energy that makes her a fun to work with. She believes in taking a simple and basic approach so that her clients could experience the success they want, taking the quickest and easiest route.

Hearn has written numerous articles/essays on time management, and she is a regular contributor to many publications and publishes her own newsletter, 'Empowering You', read by over 8000 subscribers. Hearn has also written and sold information products such as e-books and e-courses. She has the number 1 time management coaching website on Google, Yahoo and MSN worldwide, and this was achieved with her extensive internet and marketing experience.

Hearn has written many articles on time management tips in almost all the areas other experts have written. She has been engaged in conducting seminars, workshops and coaching on time management and personal development issues by many public and private sector organisations. She enjoys the credit of developing The Four Ds of Time Management, which requires a time manager to look at the tasks that need doing and decide how to handle them.

These four Ds of time management are: (I) **Do it**: anything that cannot wait and needs to be taken care of immediately. (ii) **Delegate it**: anything that might not be for the best use of your time, which you can pass it on to someone else to do. (iii) **Dump it**: anything that is unimportant now and in the future, which you can put in a bin! (iv) **Defer it**: something for the 'to do' or keep-in-view (KIV) pile, which you can come back to it later.

Another expert who has contributed some professional write ups to the subject matter of time management is Margaret Spencer Dixon, the founder and President of Spencer Consulting (www.TimeManagementFo rKawyers.com). She is a lawyer as well as a consultant who specialises in conducting time management seminars and coaching for lawyers and legal professionals.

One of her influential articles, published in the American Bar Association's Lawyering Skills Bulletin, Vol 3(2), was entitled: "Time Management: An Essential Skill for the Successful Lawyer". In this article, she argues that the lawyers' ability to manage their time effectively affects the quality of their legal work, the quality of their services to their clients and their general job satisfaction. She recommends that lawyers should ensure effective utilisation of their time so as to enhance their chances of success in their professional career given the current competitive legal environment.

Janice Cuny of the University of Oregon, New Zealand is another expert on time management who has been organising workshops and seminars to different groups of participants. She specialises in addressing time management in the context of balancing career with family issues. Notable mentoring workshops organized by her, that have been captured in the literature, were those held in 1993, 1994, and 1999 for various groups of women academics working in some universities.

In an essay entitled: "Time Management and Family Issues", which was a summary of the latest mentoring workshop organised for new women academics, Cuny concludes that women at all stages of their careers—from novice faculty members to eminently successful senior women—struggle with the substantial demands that compete for their time. She argues that time management should be considered a skill every woman academic need to cultivate throughout her career. Being a faculty member is time consuming at any stage in a woman's academic career. This effort of Cuny is close to the main objective of this book, which is focused on the way male and female scholars should use and manage their time as they run their affairs in life.

Flashman, R. H. a specialist in resource management, with his associates like Robert J. Fetsch and Linda A. Bradley, operate a Cooperative Extension Service that addresses time management issues. Their write up on: "The Successful Person's Guide to Time Management" provides useful insights on: what is good time management; how one should evaluate him-or herself; how one should visualise his/her goals; how to handle big jobs; how to deal with technology time wasters; how one could increase his/her efficiency by 50% or more; and what to do to always have the belief that "there is enough time".

They share the belief of Dorathy Cudaback (a family life extension specialist) that time management does not mean being busy all the time - it means using your time the way you want to use it to efficiently pursue your goals in life. Their conclusion is that good time management brings with it increased relaxation, less stress, more satisfaction, and great accomplishments.

Sue W. Chapman and Michael Rupured are experts in time management who consult for the University of Georgia Cooperative Extension Services Unit. One of their master pieces that they wrote on the subject of time management was a pamphlet entitled: Ten Strategies for Better Time Management. The pamphlet, which was a product of

23

their numerous years of teaching and seminar experiences on time management, was first produced in 2008.

In that pamphlet, they argued about the following ten issues as the strategies for better time management: (I) Know How You Spend Your Time; (ii) Set Priorities, (iii) Use Planning Tools; (iv) Get Organised; (v) Schedule to time; (vi) Delegate; (vii) Stop Procrastinating; (viii) Manage External Time Wasters; (ix) Avoid Multi-tasking; (x) Stay Healthy. They gave adequate illustrative examples on how to practice each of those ten strategies.

2.3 Academic Works on Time Management Process

As stated earlier, most of the write ups in time management literature are contributed by professional time management speakers, coaches and mentors. Few academics, that use English as a medium of communication, did much rigorous research works on the subject of time or time management. This dearth of scholarly literature puts 'time' and its management at a disadvantage when it comes to recognition as a subject of study in schools, colleges and universities compared to other resources that enjoy wealth of literature. How do academics conceptualise time and time management? How do they consider time management as field of study whose various aspects deserve theoretical framework and deep empirical studies?

To Lakein (1973), time management could be described as ability to show flexibility, to balance up activities or to exercise control over time. Simpson (1978) sees time management as a habit to be developed only through dogged determination and continuous practice, while Soucie (1986) views it as the capacity of an individual in prioritising and respecting those priorities. Schuler (1979), however, considers time management as the process by which an individual more effectively accomplishes set tasks and goals. In all these efforts the concept of "time" is dodged; it has not been explained or described!

According to Puffer (1989), many practical guides and strategies have been developed by some professionals in the field of time management to improve time management process in private and public sector organisations. This should have been supported by well established conceptual, theoretical frameworks that should guide the conduct of authoritative empirical researches on various aspects of time management.

Macan (1994) feels that lack of time is a common complaint in western society, prompting many responses from management scientists on how time should be effectively managed to deal with its perceived scarcity. There is a proliferation of books, essays, articles, workshops and seminars on time management in the general field of management, but these efforts are mainly done with the western society mindset. The efforts are done mainly to find ways of improving the efficiency of management and employees of organisations, rather than on the need to develop conceptual framework, theoretical framework or to promote empirical research work in the field of time management.

The fact that time management (not just 'time') lacks a universally accepted definition is an issue that Perry (1997) considers as very serious and fundamental. Despite the numerous time management training, coaching and public speaking going on all over the world, mainly conducted by motivational speakers, there is lack of universal agreement as to what exactly is time management.

Jex & Elacqua (1999) conclude that only a modest amount of empirical research has been conducted in the area of time management despite the fact that the value of time management skills and behaviors enjoys widespread acceptance. It is unfortunate that research institutes/organisations and relevant professional bodies are not doing much to ensure that time management process enjoys the research attention it deserves.

According to Hellsten (2005), there is lack of a theoretical model of time management and, it is clear that absence of a well established theoretical background is a very serious minus to the development of any field of study. Hellsten (2005) argues that there has been no published psychometric review or comparison of instruments being purported by many experts for self-reporting on the effectiveness of time management. These instruments need to be critically reviewed for different environments, organisations, races, gender, ages, level of economic development, etc before coming up with the best instruments that should enjoy global acceptance for adaption and adoption. This is an academic challenge worth overcoming to promote time management as a field of study.

Apart from this conceptual deficiency, there is also a dearth of theoretical and empirical literature in the field of time management. Few works are done theoretically and empirically on the various aspects of time management: meanings, uses and users, effectiveness, instruments for assessment/evaluation, research guide/methodology, impact to industry or government, etc.

Claessens, et al (2007) had the purpose of providing an overview for those interested in continuing with the current state-of-the-art in time management research. Although the paper demonstrates that time management behaviors relate positively to perceived control of time, job satisfaction, and healthy wellbeing, and negatively to stress, the paper also confirms that no single universally acceptable definition of time management exists, likewise a theory on time management is lacking. According to the paper, questions like "how does time management work and why?" is still universally unanswered in the literature. What a challenge to management science scholars!

McNamara (2010)'s concern was on the time management behaviors of managers of small scale businesses, and the factors that influence the behaviors, especially in the Australian economy in which the paper reported that there were 1.93 million active small businesses as at 2009. In the paper, Rudd (2009) was cited to have reported that: small scale businesses in Australia constitute 96% of all businesses in that country, contribute 35% to the GDP, employ 3.8 million people and account for around 46% of total private sector employment. The contribution of small scale businesses, being the bedrock to economic development of all developed economies of the world, deserves the attention of management science scholars so as to appreciate the factors that impact positively on their growth.

The paper develops a model that captures five factors that influence small business managers' time management behaviors in Australia, which include: organisational characteristics, personal characteristics, information technology, work life balance and external environment. The model also captures four time management behaviors being influenced, which are: setting goals and prioritising activities, the mechanics of time management, performance for being organised and perceived control of time.

The paper argues that many small business managers are successful not just because they have the right products, but mainly because they have strong work ethics and excellent time management skills. It is, therefore, desirable for small scale business owners and managers to acquire time management skills before even starting the business and then continue to improve on the skills through continuous training, so as to avoid the high incidences of failures among small scale businesses all over the world.

In what might be considered as a serious critique to the scanty literature on time management, Hellsten (2012) made effort to describe the state of time management literature and the rationale for time management training, including the audience for whom the time management literature is written. The aim of the study was, therefore, to "comprehensively review existing published and peer-reviewed literature relating to the concept of time management in order to delineate the skills and behaviors associated with time management identified in the education, industrial, administrative, management, coaching, and sport and exercise psychology domains".

Being a literature review work, Hellsten (2012) located articles and books using both database searches (e.g., ERIC, ProQuest Education, PSYCHINFO, etc.) and manual reviews of references. Keywords used in the search included time, time management, time management skills, time management behaviors, time management training programs, time management questionnaire, time management instruments, planning, scheduling, and organising. For the first, second and third searches made, using different approaches and keywords, the paper reported the acquisition of around 100 empirical peer reviewed papers as well as generic and popular books and articles that are purely on time management. Majority of the write ups obtained are not research based, as among the 100 located articles related to time management, only 38 were empirical studies involving qualitative or quantitative time management research.

Hellsten (2012) concludes by observing that "despite the widespread use of the term time management, there is currently no universally accepted definition of time management and no agreement regarding the skills and behaviors that constitute time management". But the review conducted has proved that the need to effectively use time in all undertakings has long been recognised as a crucial factor for success.

Writing on the techniques for time management, Zerihun & Krishna (2012) aim to find out techniques for solving the problems of time management for all those people holding executive or managerial positions in public and private sector organisations, and who are charged with getting things done and achieving results. The paper examines the different dimensions of time management for improving effectiveness and efficiency within the organisations.

The paper argues for seven steps to set priorities in life for effective management of time to achieve individual and organisational objectives: (I) decide exactly what we want (goal); (ii) write it down; (iii) set a deadline for achieving the goal; (iv) list out what must be done to achieve the goal; (v) organise the list into an execution plan; (vi) take action plan immediately; and (vii) resolve to do something every day that moves you towards your major goal. The paper is of the view that a good time manager's principle should always be: Proper Prior Planning Prevents Poor Performance and saves time:

Zerihun & Krishna (2012) also emphasise on some benefits of effective time management which, according to the paper, are: greater productivity, efficiency and effectiveness; more focus to one's efforts; more likely to achieve various objectives; more likely to be able to develop a job long term; more satisfaction and enjoyment from what one does; and finding that home, family and job responsibilities fit better together.

Afful-Broni (2013) investigates the time management behavior of academic and administrative staff of the University of Education, Winneba, Ghana. A total sample of 87 university workers, consisting of 45 males and 42 females were involved in the study. A three-part questionnaire was designed to elicit information from the respondents. It is discovered that respondents devoted much of their time to work, followed by sleep (on which most of the respondents indicated taking 4-6 hours daily) and recreation. One of the surprise findings of the study is that female administrative staff were found to be more prudent in time management behavior than male academic and administrative staff. The paper concedes to the fact that time is a reality whose definition is quite difficult to compose. It recommends that university authorities should design means of rewarding staff efforts at good time management behaviors, especially the issue of punctuality to work and other assignments. This approach would have encouraged effective time scheduling and punctuality to organised meetings, functions or events in the university system anywhere in the world.

Azar & Zafer (2013) confirm the impact of three underlying factors of time management (planning, organising and mechanics) in the setting of an emerging economy, like Pakistan. The three factors were found to be very influential in the effective management of all the activities of private and public sector organisations. To add to the problem of absence of universally acceptable definition of time management and non-existence of its underlying theory, the paper dismisses the phrase "time management" as misleading in itself. The paper's reason is that time cannot be managed because it exists as an inaccessible factor. According to the paper, it makes more sense to emphasise on self-management, even though in the management literature self-management is usually described as supervision and regulation of oneself, without any specific reference to the monitoring of time.

On time management in the educational sector, a relatively wealthy literature has been developed to guide academic staff, administrative staff and students on how they could be effective and efficient in managing their time for better running of their lives. Various dimensions of time management skills and behavior measurements have been developed by some scholars for usage in ensuring efficiency and effectiveness in the educational system. These measurements were tested by a fairly good number of scholars. All these are modest attempts at emphasising the importance of time management in the lives of all the stakeholders in the educational system.

Perhaps the educational system's stakeholders whose time management issue attracted the greatest attention of concerned time management scholars are the students. The following contributions are noted from the literature: Wratcher & Jones (1988), a time management workshop for adult learners, Macan, Shahani, Dipboye & Phillips (1990), college students' time management: correlations with academic performance and stress; Britton & Tesser (1991), effects of time-management practices on college grades; Trueman & Hartley (1996), a comparison between the time management and academic performance of mature and traditional-entry university students; Misra & McKean (2000), college students' academic stress and its relation to their anxiety, time management, and leisure satisfaction; Lahmers & Zulauf (2000), factors associated with academic time use and academic performance of college students: a recursive approach; Ho (2003), time management of final year undergraduate English projects: Supervisees' and the supervisor's coping strategies; Afful-Broni (2005), time management workshop for tertiary students; Swart, Lombard & De Jager (2010), exploring the relationship between time management skills and the academic achievement of African engineering students: a case study.

On the time management practices of teachers, educators, lecturers, instructors or researchers in the educational system, the following efforts are noticed: Kozoll (1982), time management for educators; Collins

(1987), time management for teachers: practical techniques and skills that give you more time to teach; Wachter & Carhart (2003), time-saving tips for teachers; Van de Meer, Jansen & Tarenbeek (2010), it's almost a mindset that teachers need to change: first-year students' need to be inducted into time management; Dandago (2012), time management for university lecturer: a milestone for academic excellence.

On a general community usage of time for better administration of the educational system, the following contributions are made to the literature: Shipman (1983), effective time management techniques for school administrators; Kearns & Gardiner (2007), is it time well spent? the relationship between time management behaviors, perceived effectiveness and work-related morale and distress in a university context; Afful-Broni, A. 2013), time management behavior among academic and administrative staff of the university of education, Winneba, Accra, Ghana.

2.4 Religious Perspectives of Time Management

So far, all the principles, practices, ideas and issues on time and time management are conventional or universal to followers of all faiths in the world as they are more of ethical reference than religious reference. But the whole submission might tally 100% with the teachings of one religion or another and, so, followers of those religions should comply as they manage their time as part of their religious obligations. However, it is clear that in this world of religiosity as a way of life, different religions have their different perspective to time management and the need to go by that perspective in managing the personal, official and social lives of their followers. It is, therefore, advisable that scholars should make appropriate adjustments to the time management principles, practices and ideas presented in Chapters 4-10 to suit the teachings of their religions where there is any deviation.

In Islamic faith, for example, some scholars and practitioners have contributed write ups (mainly in Arabic language) on time management from the perspective of Islam. In those write ups there might be no significant deviations from issues discussed in this book. The main difference which could be easily noted is that, while there are no religious injunctions to back up issues raised in this book, authors of write ups giving Islamic perspective to time management have to support their statements with Quranic verses or Hadith of the Prophet (PBUH) for followers to feel religiously obliged to comply.

Among those contributors to the field of time management in Islam are Jibreel (1977), Time: More Precious than All Treasures on Earth; Fahd (1988), Time Management: A Developing Approach to Success; Dale (1991), Time Management; Mohamed (1992), Time: Construction or Destruction; Khuldun (1993), Reflection on the Value of Time; Hassan (1995), Skills of Time Management; Abdullah (1996), Principles of Management and Leadership in Islam; Yusuf (1997), Time in the Muslim's Life; Mohamed (1999), More Precious Than Gold; Al-Jaraisy (2001), Time Management: An Islamic View; Jabnoun (2001), Time Efficiency in Islam; and Al-Jeraisy (2002), Time Management From Islamic and Administrative Perspective.

Jabnoun (2001) mentions that while time means money in the West, it means "Life" in Islam, and that Muslims must understand that whatever time they lose is lost from their limited life for which they are accountable to Allah. The write ups quoted the Prophet (PBUH) where he said: "Man will be asked about his life, how he spent it; his youth, how he used it, and his money, how he earned it and how he spent it". The Prophet (PBUH) was also quoted to have said: "Take advantage of five before five: your youth before your aging; your health before your sickness; your wealth before your poverty; your free time before your busy time; and your life before your death". Muslims are encouraged to be scheduling their time effectively between three main activities: seeking knowledge, formally worshiping Allah and working.

Al-Jeraisy (2002)'s contribution pertains to the definition and conceptualisation of time and time management according to the teachings of Islam, time in the glorious Qur'an, time and the purpose of creation, and time management in the glorious Qur'an in respect to the functions of management discussed in Chapter 4 (planning, organising, directing, controlling and decision making). It also covers the position of time in the Purified Sunnah, emphasising on time as a great blessing (equally endowed to mankind), time as a great responsibility, time as a vehicle for worship, encouraging effective utilisation of time and warning against wasting it. The write up also highlights the Muslim's duty regarding time and its management, to ensure that he/she benefits from time, utilises leisure time, races for good deeds, learns from the passage of time, planning and organising time and fulfilling of time commitments.

One of the few empirical works on Islamic Time management was conducted by Muhammad, et al (2011) which emphasises the need for the adoption of high level principles of time management in Islam. The paper highlights those principles that address individual, as well as collective, needs practically and intellectually in all walks of life, as per the teachings of Islam. The paper also discusses high level principles of Islam for effective time management in achieving maximum productivity, based purely on guidelines selected from the Qur'an and some sayings of Prophet Muhammad (PBUH) which are relevant to effective time management.

Prioritising, maximizing productivity by identifying specific time for specific job, hard work, planning/ setting objectives, act quickly and avoid procrastinating, leaving the irrelevant, excellence/quality work - elimination of waste, stress management, and accountability of time are the Islamic effective traits the paper suggests for incorporation in contemporary individual habits and organisational practices to increase operational efficiency and productivity.

All the contributors to the write ups on time management in Islam are emphasising on time management as a life style, since time management is expected to be done mainly to ensure strong commitment to knowledge-seeking, fear or worship of Allah, and show of commitment to means of livelihood. Time management is, therefore, a means of deriving peaceful life in this world and in the hereafter.

In Christian faith, a good number of write ups are available on time management from the perspective of Christianity, although most of the write ups are essays, popular books, and website postings by some churches. Just like the Muslim writers on time management, the Christian writers and motivational speakers on time management are also emphasising on the need to commit adequate time to the worship of God and to other religious related activities. This is the main point of deviation with the conventional/universal time management system, where general ethical issues are emphasised.

Some of the efforts made on time management from the Christian perspective are those of Harris (1999) which addresses the topic: Redeeming the Time: A Christian Perspective of Time Management; Stanley (2002) which deals with: The Seven Keys to Good Time Management in Christianity; Nickel (2003) which covers the topic Clock: The Heritage of Christian Faith; Leafe (2004) which addresses the subject of Personal Time Management in Christianity; Peach (2012) which looks at the Ten Tips for Effective Time Management in Christianity; and

Edwards (nd) emphasising on the importance of time management in the Christian life.

All the write ups have made it clear that in Christianity, time management is not about doing a lot of activities, but it is about doing the right and necessary things to accomplish personal goals and God's desire. For a Christian, it means he/she should be committed to doing things that would show his/her obedience to God's will and to the life of humanity. Edwards (nd), one of the best time managers the Church has ever seen, emphasises that for a Christian to better manage his/her time, the person must take care of the following 4 issues: (I) don't wait to get started, (ii) make time of worship and service priority, (iii) use your leisure time for spiritual and physical refreshment, and (iv) avoid all time wasters. Relevant scriptures were cited to support, or give more credibility to, the points raised.

Peach (2012) discusses ten tips for effective time management among Christian faithful, which are: put God first; know God's will; find the right priority; think; say 'no' to the unimportant; do important tasks, not just urgent ones; write things down; know what needs to be done; live as if today were your last; and plan for tomorrow. Just like all other write ups on time management in Christianity, the emphasis of any time management technique to be put in place is to prioritise God's will to personal or organisational wish.

Like their Muslims counterparts, writers on time management in Christianity are also emphasising on time management as a way of life, showing how the whole endowed time is expected to be invested in the worship of God: the home, place of work, during leisure, etc. Believers are not expected to spend a second of their time doing anything that is not in tune with the teachings of Christianity. Therefore, time management in Christianity is a learning process which, by extension, is to be practiced by the faithful as a life style!

Just as is the case with the above two dominant religions on earth (Christianity, accounting for 31.5%, and Islam, accounting for 23.2%, together constitute around 55% of the world population, according to the Pew Research Centre, 2012), other faiths, like Hinduism, Buddhism, Judaism, Sikhism, Taoists, Jainism, Baha'ism, Mormonism, Jewish, etc, might have their own various perspectives on time management. The time management principles under these perspectives need to be observed by the followers of those religions (since they must have been made part of their religious obligations). Again, the principles need to be respected by associates and neighbors who transact a number of businesses and other activities with the followers of these religions.

2.5 Moving Time Management Literature Forward

It is apparent that English-language-based time management literature has a lot of "unfortunate gaps", in view of the necessity of time and the importance of its management in all spheres of life. It is unfortunate that no clear-cut universally acceptable definition has been established for time, time management, good time management behavior, time management skills, etc. It is unfortunate that no acceptable theoretical framework has been established on time management and its various aspects. It is also unfortunate that very few empirical researches have been conducted on various aspects of time management in the public, private and NGO sectors of even the advanced economies of the world, where time management is more emphasised.

How many conferences on time management or on management science with high emphasis on time management are organised by universities, other research institutions and professional bodies annually across the world? It is almost at zero level, as per the existing literature! How many academic seminars are conducted annually in universities and other research institutes, especially management-based institutions? How much money is committed annually to research on various aspects of time management by academic institutions and professional bodies that are meant to promote management science as a necessary field of study for socio-economic development of any nation? The current literature is not handy with answers to these simple questions!

Again, the facts from the literature suggest that only a few well researched books are available on time management, but just a few well researched book chapters; almost zero theses/dissertations on time management are produced by universities and other research institutes; almost zero programmes of studies leading to award of degrees or diplomas on time management exist; and there is near absence of courses in degree/diploma programmes of universities and other research institutes. This calls for immediate concerns of the relevant authorities particularities management based universities and management professional bodies, especially those that use English language as a medium of instruction.

It is in response to all the above short-comings that the Universiti Utara Malaysia (UUM), being an eminent management university, through its publication unit, the UUM Press, requested for the production of this book, after a Public Lecture on the subject matter was organised by the School of Accountancy (SOA), College of Business (COB) of the university. The book is designed to achieve two broad objectives: (i) to address how all scholars in the universities system and beyond should be effectively managing their time and (ii) to challenge scholars, especially those in the field of management science, to embark on researches on various "virgin" areas of time management so as to promote it in theory and practice.

A modest bibliographical list is developed at the end of the book to facilitate the achievement of objective 2! The list provides a fairly good reference for any research work to be conducted in the area of time management.

CHAPTER THREE

WHO IS A SCHOLAR?

3.1 Scholar Concept

A scholar is a person who is sincerely committed to knowledge production activities in an academic institution.

Sincerity, which is an ethical issue, must be seen in the academic work a person does before he/she is accepted as a scholar; commitment to the plight of scholarship as a discipline is equally important in defining a scholar; the person must be a very good and/or an excellent producer of knowledge on a continuous basis for him/her to be accepted as a scholar; and the person must be attached to an academic institution. In summary, a scholar is any person who shows sincerity, commitment and respect for scholarship as he/she produces knowledge on a continuous basis in an academic institution.

Knowledge production activities are constant readings (of books, journals, magazines, newspapers, newsletters, pamphlets, internet posts, authoritative reports, etc) to remain current in the chosen field of study; conduct of research on continuous basis (through survey and other means of gathering primary and secondary data); giving lectures, seminars, workshops, symposia, talks, etc to students of knowledge in the chosen field of study on a consistent basis; writing and publishing articles, books, internet posts, etc to disseminate acquired knowledge and to promote the application of an acquired idea, model, theory, etc for the betterment of humanity; and involvement in community services to ensure societal growth and development using endowed knowledge.

An academic institution could be a University, Polytechnic, College, Research Institute, Secondary School (or equivalent), Primary/Basic School (or equivalent), etc. A scholar uses any of these as his/her base to produce quality knowledge for the use of humanity belonging to the present and future generations.

Being a scholar is one of the best achievements a person could make in life and it carries with it a lot of responsibilities, which are further described in this Chapter. For simplicity of understanding, many educational institutions, particularly universities, condense the responsibilities a scholar into three categories: Research, Teaching and Community Services. These responsibilities compete for the limited time available to a serious scholar!

3.2 A scholar as Researcher

A good scholar is a person who masters how to conduct qualitative research, quantitative research and a combination of the two (the qual-quan research), or at least any one of the two general approaches of conducting research. The person masters the epistemology and methodology of research.

Epistemology is the "theory or science of the grounds of acquiring knowledge" (OED 2004). If a scholar wants to produce knowledge then he/she has to rely on an implicit or explicit epistemology. According to Chua (1986), while epistemology refers to the principles of knowledge acquisition, methodology refers to ways of acquiring it. Some of the principles of knowledge acquisition are obedience, perseverance, patience, humility, integrity, due mutual respect, etc.

While epistemology deals with the question of what knowledge is and the grounds of acquiring it, methodology deals with how valid knowledge can be acquired. Methodology is, therefore, about the study of methods (Mingers, 2001), and it analyses the different methods used in research. The most important divide between research methods is that between quantitative and qualitative methods. A good scholar appreciates this fact a lot, and carries this appreciation along while conducting research on a continuous basis.

Ethical issues of integrity, honesty, independence, objectivity, confidentiality and competence are to be demonstrated by a scholar while conducting any type of research. Specifically, all researches should be free from the following ethical problems: plagiarism, and even self-plagiarism; falsification of results/data; harming the subjects or misrepresentation of respondents' position; poor literature review; and incompetence in the topic chosen for research.

As a research is conducted, next is for the output to be published in the best interest of humanity. The publication could be through the media of an academic or professional journal, book or book chapter, magazine, newsletter, newspaper, pamphlet, authoritative report, web posting, etc.

A good scholar takes the pain of satisfying the guidelines/requiremen ts for publication of articles in journals, especially the top ranking journals in his/her field of study, developing a strong shock-absorber for the likelihood of rejection of contributed article after passing through rigorous blind review. The scholar also invests in contributing publication fee to non-CSR journals in which he/she would want to have his/her accepted articles published.

Also, the epistemology principle of patience is exercised by a good scholar to allow room for all the processes of review, acceptance, and publication to take their natural course on submission made of an article for journal or manuscript for a book. Some journals are published twice or once in a year, as they have very rigorous review processes.

It is a general belief in the academic that journal articles promote scholars (publish or perish), while books make them popular!

Beside publication of journal articles, books, etc, a good scholar also disseminates knowledge through conference/seminar attendance (local and international). All over the world, conferences/seminars are held in all fields of study to showcase new developments, new research findings, and new models in the field of study. A good scholar is he/she that attends those conferences to share new knowledge and network with other scholars from across the world.

A good scholar might not wait for sponsorship to attend knowledge production conferences/seminars that are very useful to his/her career development; covering the cost of attendance is treated as an investment by a serious scholar! If sponsorship is available, however, the scholar applies for it, based on the specified criteria.

At the conference/seminar, a good scholar would want to make his/her impact being felt by sharing his/her knowledge in a humble manner; by asking questions on presentations made which are not clear to him/her, with politeness; and by establishing new friends and contacts. To a good scholar, conference/seminar attendance (local or international) is a project that demands investment of appropriate time, money and other resources.

3.3 A Scholar as Teacher

A scholar is a good teacher, teaching the students what he/she knows or understand for them to understand even better than him/her! He/she shows commitment in teaching his undergraduate and postgraduate students (for scholars in the university system), or teaching senior or junior classes (for scholars at the primary or secondary school levels). A good scholar takes his class teaching as a very serious business transaction, demanding a lot of time for reading of new knowledge to give to the students, preparation of the lecture/lesson outline and how to successfully present the lecture/lesson, approach of testing the class understanding of the lecture/lesson delivered and how to incorporate that lecture/lesson into the final examination question, all within the limited time for each class.

So, before, during and after each class, a serious scholar thinks of the time to invest in the best interest of the students. If the lecture period is 2 hours, how much time is needed for its preparation and for post-lecture review? More time is invested in the pre-lecture preparation by a serious scholar than during the lecture!

Effective and successful lecture delivery does not stand and end with the contact in the class; the whole exercise starts with syllabus mastery, to subject mastery (reading as many books as possible relevant to the subject), to lesson/lecture note preparation (including the need for progress testing at the end of each class), to the actual class delivery and interaction, to past-lecture review, to preparation of questions paper, marking scheme for internal and external moderation, to conduct of examination and compilation of continuous assessment scores, to marking of the examination scripts and compilation of total scores to submission of results of the students performance to vetting by the appropriate authorities. What a time consuming task!

It is when the above processes are thrown away that much time would not be seen to be going to class teaching, and the person involved should not be accepted as a scholar at all. In fact the person manipulating teaching responsibility to have more time for himself/herself should be seen as someone not genuine (a quack), a fraudulent person!

Supervision (or monitoring) of students and their academic works, like thesis, dissertation or research project works is part of the teaching responsibilities of a scholar. A good scholar would budget a lot of time for reading through the works or write ups of his/her supervisees, for contact with them to exchange ideas and strike understanding with the work being done, and for rehearsal where the work needs to be presented somewhere for assessment or examination. To a good scholar, supervisor-supervisee relationship is a contractual relationship that demands demonstration of moral soundness, care, concern and sense of belonging. It needs some time out of the limited time available to a scholar.

Closely related to the issue of supervision, as a responsibility of a scholar, is the need for a scholar to commit some precious time to mentor his/her students. A good scholar sees himself/herself as a mentor to all his/her students.

The mentor, a more prominent or influential person, guides, protects, and promotes the mentee's career, training, and overall wellbeing. A mentee is, therefore, one whose welfare, training, or career is promoted by an influential person (i.e. mentor). The mentee (student in this case) is, therefore, the subject of the mentor (the scholar in our own case), who needs the time of the mentor for guidance, linkage and promotion to many opportunities for growth and development in chosen career.

'Mentoring' has become a universal term to describe benefits implicit in professional organisation memberships, graduate programs, and workplace environments. Mentorship practice has been part of the human experience since the Golden Age of Greece. Engaging with a mentor as a way to learn and achieve one's full potential is an ancient and respected practice. A scholar must have passed through some degree of mentorship before he/she becomes established. There is, therefore, the need for the same service to be extended to the students as future generation of scholars.

3.4 A Scholar as Community Servant

A scholar belongs to a number of communities, and they all need the services of that person.

First is the immediate family community, consisting of wife, husband, children. There are extended family members, like grandfathers, grandmothers of both husband and wife; uncles, cousins, nieces, aunties, etc are members of the extended immediate community. There are childhood and other closed friends and classmates, who see themselves as part of the immediate family members' to a scholar.

They all need the time of the scholar for household routine activities, marital responsibilities, some outing with the children, family meetings, visitations, social activities (marriage, naming ceremonies, condolence, etc). All these social/community services should be reasonably provided by a serious scholar, and they definitely cost some precious time!

In the university system, for example, a scholar must think and act as a member of the university community. Hence, he might be assigned some responsibilities that would definitely demand a lot of his/her time. Apart from the class reaching and students' supervision responsibility, a scholar might be appointed heads of his/her department, which would mean serving as the chief academic, administrative and financial officer

41

of the department. How much time would be left for him/her after taking care of these responsibilities sincerely?

The scholar could be appointed as a University Management/ Council Committee Chair or Member, Dean of a Faculty or School, Coordinator of a programme, Examinations Officer (at the University, Faculty/School or Departmental level), Director of a directorate, Deputy Vice Chancellor (DVC) or Vice Chancellor (VC). The scholar is expected to combine any of the responsibilities mentioned here with those of research, teaching, conference attendance, students' supervision, family responsibilities, etc. What a necessity for effective time management!

The scholar could also be spotted for a responsibility at the larger community (local government, state government or central government level and even at the continental or global levels). A scholar could be appointed a UNO, World Bank or AU Regional Director/Officer, Minister, Commissioner, Director, Controller, Coordinators, etc at various levels of the larger community because of the confidence reposed in him/her by the relevant authority. As any of these larger community responsibilities is discharged, the scholar is expected to remain committed to knowledge production and dissemination. This would demand high degree of time management!

3.5 Learning as a Lifestyle

The foregoing submission on a scholar shows that the responsibilities of a scholar, as a human being, are enormous. This suggests that a scholar is arguably in the most demanding condition to make it a point of necessity to effectively manage time for the achievement of desired results. In fact, educational institutions should make effective time management a part of the Key Performance Indicators (KPI) for assessing or appraising the quality of scholars' contributions to knowledge advancement for the purpose of promotion, awards and grants to be accorded the scholars.

A scholar is, therefore, expected to imbibe the culture of 'learning as a lifestyle' - always thinking and acting on knowledge production and dissemination to advance the cause of humanity, using the limited time available. This is, incidentally, the culture expected to be imbibed by all the staff and students of UUM, as an eminent management University.

A true scholar remains a student and servant of knowledge until the end of his/her life!

CHAPTER FOUR

CONTEXTUALISING TIME MANAGEMENT

4.1 The Concept of Time

The term 'time' has been defined as "the passing of all the days, months and years, taken as a whole" (Hornby, 1998: 740). This definition was improved by Hornby (2010:765) where time is defined as: "Indefinite continued progress of existence and events in the past, present and future, regarded as a whole." This means that time is the indicator of the situation in the past, the present and the future. We do everything within available time, and this time shapes events and flies away - very fast!

Time could be defined in terms of second, minute, hour, day, week, month, year, decade, generation or century. It is a gift from God, which does not remain static as it moves on, even as the owner (endowee) decides to stay on. It is an endowment to humanity for the discharge of numerous responsibilities assigned by the endower (God). Its management becomes more delicate and complicated as human beings decide to create 'self-interest' responsibilities to discharge within the limited time endowed.

Time, as a resource, is needed for all we do in life and, so, no matter how well a person plans to use other resources, he/she must plan for the influence of time in achieving his/her objectives. Where there is no time, all other resources become useless!

As stated earlier, time is the only resource God endowed on people equally. What is greatly needed for humanity to do, with the limited time, is to effectively manage it in accomplishing set tasks.

Scholars are part of humanity facing the challenges of time management, based on the peculiarities of their numerous responsibilities.

4.2 The Concept of Time Management

Time management is found to be suffering from universally acceptable definition and, so, it is hereby defined as the process of time planning, organising, directing and controlling by any time conscious user. Time management is necessary for whatever one does in life and for continuous improvement in performance of whatever activity one undertakes. The term is also about utilising time effectively to achieve individual and organisational goals/objectives.

Time management is to be pursued with all vigor in private and public lives and at whatever level of organisational structure of governmental and non-governmental organisations. This is due to the simple fact that time is always not enough to cover all the activities intended by anybody or any organisation.

Time management demands the deployment of all the functions of management, making time the focus of analysis, to show how a time manager should effectively utilise time for the achievement of set goals and objectives. The four main functions of management to be taken care of by a good scholar, acting as good time manager, are: planning, organising, directing and controlling. For scholars to earn respect in carrying around the message 'learning is their lifestyle', they must prove that they are excellent "time managers", showing effectiveness in time management. They also have to bear in mind that dealing away with 'time wasters' is necessary for achieving academic excellence!

To perform well as a scholar, one has to show effectiveness in the management of the resources at his/her disposal, the most important of which is "time". Effective management requires demonstration of good appreciation and practice of management functions: planning, organising, directing and controlling. These functions are to be applied on "time" for it to be seen as well managed.

4.3 A Scholar as Time Planner

Planning is the first and probably the most important of the functions of management since the success or failure of a management depends directly or indirectly on proper planning. Planning could be seen as today's design for tomorrow's action (Garba, 2001). It could be viewed as what to do, how to do it, why, where, who and when to do it. Planning is in fact a pre-condition for the survival of any individual or organisation.

Plans should be precise, practicable and easy; they should be flexible and based on facts. Plans can be conceptualised from a number of different perspectives. They may be differentiated in terms of the time horizon (short-range and long-range), the scope of activities represented (strategic and operational) and the specific uses to which they are put or with respect to their frequency of use.

In time management, a scholar is expected to be precise and concise as he/she plan to use the next second, minute, hour, day, week, month, year, etc. One is not too sure whether or not he/she would live to see the event planned for, but reasonableness must be exercised in planning for the utilisation of the future time.

This function of management suggests that a good scholar, who is expected to be a good time planner, should be very good in budgeting and budgetary control, forecasting the future, estimation of happenings, standard setting as well as variance analysis on time utilisation.

4.4 A Scholar as Time Organiser

Organising is the process of identifying and grouping of the work to be performed, defining and delegating responsibility and authority and establishing relationships for the purpose of enabling people to work together effectively in accomplishing objectives (Druker, 1964),. A good scholar is a good organiser of resources and, so, time should be given top priority as the function of organising is discharged.

It is undisputable to say that people would do better when they know what is expected of them as a team, hence the concept of "synergy". Scholars are known as synergy generators as they usually work as a team for research, teaching and other academic and professional activities. This culture assists scholars to make effective utilisation of their time and save a lot for other important activities.

This function of management suggests that a good scholar, who is expected to be a good time organiser, should be very good in identification of responsibilities to be charged and by who, grouping/teaming of colleagues or students to discharge a responsibility optimally, delegation of responsibility that might be more economical to discharge by a lower level person and controlling of activities to ensure that synergy is achieved within the limited time available.

4.5 A Scholar as Time Director

Directing is about motivating and guiding subordinates towards achieving organisational objectives. From the perspective of time management, a scholar is expected to ensure that all the students and colleagues working with him or under his control are effectively directed as to what they should do so that his/her time is not affected by their actions or inactions.

This demands commanding from the part of the scholar as a time manager. Commanding is dependent upon three variables, i.e. communication skills, leadership and motivation. Communication could be defined as the achievement of meaning and understanding between people through verbal and non-verbal means in order to affect behavior and achieve desired results Druker, 1967),. This is a very essential element in management because "communication gap" is always the root cause of most individual and organisational problems. A good scholar should avoid it as much as possible.

Leadership, on the other hand, can be summarized as the ability to guide, direct, conduct, persuade or influence people to perform a given task voluntarily in order to attain a given goal (Quarshie, 2002). A good scholar is assumed to be a good academic leader, who should demonstrate the abilities specified here as the person manages all resources, especially time.

As a scholar works with lower level staff and students, appropriate measures should be taken to motivate them to put in their best for the achievement of the desired goals/objectives, within the specified time. A good scholar, as a good time manager, is also expected to be a good motivator!

This function of management suggests that a good scholar, who is expected to be a good time director, should be very good in motivation, supervision, mentoring, commanding, coordination, leadership, communication, harmonisation and synergising towards set goals/objectives within the available time.

4.6 A Scholar as Time Controller

Controlling is a mechanism used to ensure that activities stay on course or remain in conformity with desired plans. When time is planned/ budgeted, there is need for measures of control to be adopted to ensure that there is no unnecessary deviation as the activities are discharged. A scholar is to ensure this, if he/she is to be accepted as a good time manager.

Control, which is a continuous process, involves measuring actual results of performance in relation to the desired results and taking corrective action when necessary. Planned activities and timing are to be compared with the actual results obtained, and any variance arising in the time specified should be subjected to investigation before reaching conclusion as to whether the variance is favorable or unfavorable.

46

Controlling, therefore, is a measure taken by time manager at the end of the planning period.

This function of management suggests that a good scholar, who is expected to be a good time controller, should be very good in coordination, supervision, liaison, enforcement and other control measures.

4.7 A Scholar as Timely Decision Maker

All the functions of management which a scholar, as a good time manager, is expected to discharge, are not ends in themselves, but rather means to an end. This is because, the main responsibility of a time manager is decision making on how the available time is to be utilised, why it should be utilised in a particular way, where it is to be utilised, when it should be utilised, who are to be responsible for its utilisation, etc.

When a scholar, as a time manager, persistently makes good time management related decisions, he/she is praised/commended by superiors, colleagues and other stakeholders, but when the reverse is the case, it is almost certain that he/she would be condemned/criticised by many people.

In view of this, adherence to the functions of management (planning, organising, directing and controlling) to ensure effective time management and utilisation by scholars will go a long way in improving the quality of their decisions as academic leaders and chief administrators of the their research communities, and would definitely ensure that the qualities of their researches, teachings and community services are on the high side.

CHAPTER FIVE

SCARCITY OF TIME

5.1 Basic Cause of the Scarcity

A scholar, as a human being, needs time for working, eating, learning, meeting, traveling, worshipping, playing, resting, sleeping, researching, writing, etc. Eating, travelling, worshipping, playing/socialising, resting and sleeping are not part of the three time-consuming responsibilities of a scholar, as discussed in Chapter 3. But these activities compete for a substantial share of the limited time available to that person. They succeed in getting much of the limited time available to a scholar, in many cases more than 50% of it!

Generally speaking, the twenty-four hours in a day, the seven days in a week, the four weeks in a month and the twelve months in a year are always not enough to cover ALL the activities intended by a serious and committed scholar in a day, week, month or year. Why?

The basic reason is that while the time frame is limited, the activities (wants) to be performed within the time frame are unlimited and, so, time will never be enough to cover all the intended activities of a serious person, like a scholar. Some of the activities are natural, while some are created by the life ambitions of a person and when you aggregate them all, they are bound to go beyond what the limited time could take. For this reason most human beings (including scholars) complain about scarcity of time.

Time is so scarce that you might hear a "busy man/woman" saying that he/she would wish a day to be made up of forty hours (Dandago, 1998, 2000, 2002, 2012, 2014)!

5.2 Other Causes of Time Scarcity

Apart from the basic cause described in 5.1, which is applicable to all scholars as human beings, there are other causes of scarcity of time which are specific to some time users, making them unable to cover all their intended activities despite their elaborate and reasonable plans. They are as follows:

49

5.2.1 Meeting unexpected visitors: (or poor time managers) is a specific/peculiar cause of scarcity of time in some cultures. At the home or place of work, when one is deeply committed to observing his/her time budget, some friends, relations and customers might interrupt by paying him/her visit without any prior notice of the visit. As they interrupt your time scheduling for that scheduled period, you would not be able to accomplish what you plan to do during that time, and as you try to forge ahead you are bound to realise that time is not enough to cover all the intended activities. Serious time managers would not entertain visitors if they have not been given appointments earlier for the visits. But caution must be exercised, as there are visitors that might feel too big to seek appointment from an officer or relation before paying him/her a visit in the office or home!

5.2.2 Poor prioritising of activities: is another cause of scarcity of time. If one does not care to define his/her priorities clearly, and pursue them accordingly, much time might be wasted away on things that are not serious in the achievement of set goals of the individual or his/her organisation. As serious and important activities to the socio-economic life of a person are not discharged during the time available, the same person might be heard complaining that time is too scarce!

5.2.3 Poor time consciousness: This is about carelessness to plan (budget) available time (second, minute. hour, day, etc) to show how it would be actually utilised. It is also about being unmindful on the way time is going, especially if not much benefits are derived from its usage. Another dimension of it is being insensitive to the need to account for the time used. A poor time conscious scholar is always unorganised, confused and an irresponsible person who should not be in the academic system in the first place!

5.2.4 Infrastructural problems: have to do with poor supply of utilities like electricity, tap born water, road network, transportation system, security system, judicial system, etc. Absence or poor supply of these utilities/services affects the time management effort of many scholars and other users in developing economies where the utilities are in short supply. As one plans to work in the night, power/electricity blackout is enough to discourage that person from carrying on with the plan, and by the next day he/she would have other things on his plate!

When water is not sufficiently available in a scholar's place of residence, he/she has to spend some times making efforts to get it from other places; when roads are bad, the users have to move very slowly to save their tyres and other accessories from damaging, spending a lot of time for that; when the judicial system is bad, plaintiff have to take too long time waiting for judgments to be passed; when security system is bad, a lot of provisions have to be made for self-defense/protection, which must affect time usage, etc.

When infrastructural facilities are poorly provided in a community, time management would be seriously affected as risks and uncertainties of their failures would be high, and these make time planning and controlling activities/mechanisms to fail woefully! Scholars are part of the larger society; they suffer the pain of the absence or poor supply of these facilities just like other members of the society. The pain is more inflicting on them as it affects their time management and utilisation efforts, which ultimately affect their productivity!

5.2.5 Natural Causes: like death of a relation and natural disaster, which would interrupt time management process and make time to appear scarce. When a scholar is sick, the whole process of time management on all his/her activities must stop, depending on the seriousness of his/her illness, until recovery. At the time of sickness, the concern is on survival and not on productivity of the scholar. By the time he/she recovers from the sickness, a lot of time that could have been used to advance research, teaching and community service must have been lost and, so, the "complain game" on time scarcity continues!

The sickness could be on the spouse of the scholar, parent, children and other close relations that would demand the attention and care of the scholar. Time must, therefore, be diverted from initial plans and be committed to caring for the sick relation, until recovery. Again, by the time that person recovers and get discharged from the hospital, the "nursing scholar" must have lost a lot of time that could be used for some academic and administrative activities.

When a relation of a scholar (spouse, child, parent, close friend/associate, etc) dies, most of the planned activities of the scholar must be suspended to pay attention to the protocols of redemption of the corpse, burial arrangement and execution, responding to condolence visits and messages, etc. These would take days, weeks or months, depending on the caliber of the dead person or the bereaved. So, as this

51

quantity of time is lost in the process, the scholar must be complaining of scarcity of time to carry on with his/her planned activities before the death.

Natural disasters like earthquakes, floods/tsunamis, fire outbreaks, etc are so devastating that when they affect a scholar, the negative impact could extend to his/her time, as resources, so much so that he/she would be complaining that time is scarce as efforts are made to recover from the trauma of the lost resources to the disaster, especially time. All time management processes on scholarly activities must come to a halt when disaster strikes a scholar, as attention is rechanneled towards survival, recovery, and condolence as well as overcoming the inflicted trauma.

5. 3 What Should Scholars Do?

The fact that time, as a very important resource, is scarce when compared with the numerous activities of a scholar, is enough reason why scholars should learn to effectively manage it for their very own benefit and for the benefits of their students and their universities/research institutions, colleges or schools. Their ability to manage the scarcity of time would make positive impact in their lives and in the well being of their universities, research centers/institutes, colleges or schools.

Effective management of the scarcity of time is particularly necessary for those scholars who find themselves in an environment where causes of scarcity of time (as described above) are enormous. Consultation with experts would pay if those causes of scarcity of time appear overwhelming to, especially, uprising/growing scholars.

An important way of dealing with the above causes of scarcity of time is effective delegation to competent subordinates (if available) so that the work of a scholar does not stop if any of the issues raised happens. Given the current influence of technology, a serious scholar should not allow his/her work to come to a standstill or die off just like that; he/she should always look for a way out so as "to keep the going go"!

CHAPTER SIX

TIME AUDIT AND ITS NECESSITY

6.1 Taking Time to Save Time

The first measure in managing time is to establish just where it has gone and how. Unless you know what is going away at the moment and how, you might not be able to take the appropriate steps to save time. The way to find out is to conduct a personal time audit. This requires taking time to save time.

Conventional *financial statements audit* is defined as an independent examination of, and the expression of an opinion on, the financial statements of an entity, by an appointed auditor, in accordance with his terms of engagement and in compliance with statutory regulations and professional requirements (Dandago, 2003). This shows that auditing is an examination, which is done independently by an appointed auditor, with a view to expressing professional opinion, based on findings, in accordance with agreed terms, and in compliance with some laws/regulations and professional requirements.

Following this definition, we can describe time audit as an independent examination of how time is utilised over a period of time, by the time owner, in accordance with his/her principles of life with a view to expressing opinion on the extent of utilisation and benefits derived so that time savings could be made in the future. This shows that time audit is conducted by the time owner (time manager) herself/himself, and reports the findings to self, and that the primary objective of the audit is to find areas where time savings could be made in the future. Hence, taking time to save time!

Time audit exercise needs a lot of discipline if the best results are to be achieved. Failure to conduct it results to great negative consequences to the life of the supposed time manager, especially a scholar. This is an issue that demands empirical studies on different categories of time users, from different sectors of diverse economies, to find out the degree of consequences of time audit failing in practical terms.

Time Audit, as expected of a scholar to show sound time management, goes with some procedures, and these are discussed as follows:

6.2 Finding out How Time Goes Out

Finding out how a time manager's time passes away requires the conduct of an effective time usage scrutiny. It should be conducted as follows:

a. Take a typical day and analyse it in details describing, mentally or in a written form (like in a time diary), what you do at certain intervals, e.g. from 7: 00 am to 9:00 am to 11:00 am to 1:00 pm, etc. This is an example of a two-hour scrutiny. It could be based on a one-hour scrutiny, five-hour scrutiny, etc. All activities conducted are to be noted down for critical analysis based on impact of the activities to the achievement of personal and organisational goals/objectives.

b. Take a week and analyse each day in a more general term, detailing what you are doing, once again at certain intervals. Every weekend the audit is to be conducted based on daily activities conducted by the time manager, emphasising on the time consumed by each identified activity and how saving could be made as time is planned to be used the next week.

c. Determine the activities that normally consume most of your time (as a social individual) and the time set for your research, teaching and community services, as a scholar.These activities are usually conducted to facilitate the achievement of your personal goals and those of your organisation.

d. Once the activities that normally and abnormally consume the time of a scholar are determined, appropriate measures should be immediately taken to save much time to be utilised in discharging other important scholarly responsibilities in the future.

At the end of the day (maybe when a scholar goes to bed, or whenever a scholar takes to be end of his/her day), there is the need for the scholar to analyse how much time he/she has spent on each category of activities. He/she can work out (mentally or in written form the percentage of a day consumed by each category of activities. This would make the scholar to monitor his/her time utilisation more effectively and serve as a motivation for improvement in his/her time management efforts in the future.

6.3 Time Consumers to a Scholar

The following are the major activities (time consumers) that must be allocated reasonable time in the life of a scholar:

6.3.1 Sleeping: This is the highest state of resting. Every normal person must create time to sleep in the morning, afternoon, evening or night, depending on circumstances. Most normal persons, however, sleep more in the night. Some people divide their sleeping time to 60%-70% in the night and the balance (40%-30%) in the afternoon. However, this percentage is not a proven theory, but just an assumption. People do practice different sleeping habits, but a scholar should go for a reasonable practice.

To rest well after physically or mentally exhausting oneself, there is the need to sleep well so that all the body system takes a full and re-energising rest. A scholar, as a good time manager should, however, be reasonable in allocating time for sleeping. It is, therefore, advisable that the aggregate time to spend on sleeping in a day should not be more than six (6) hours for an adult scholar (but there is need to refer to the acceptable sleeping chart according to age and state of health, as provided by health experts). To a serious scholar, any second more than the optimum sleeping time should be treated as a waste!

Six hours means ¼ of the whole day and, so, a scholar is to use just ¾ of the day, which is 18 hours, to take care of the numerous activities described in Chapter 3 and many more. It is clearly an indication of poor commitment to scholarship for a supposedly scholar to be sleeping for more than 6 hours (or any defined reasonable time) in a day, unless if he/she is sick!

6.3.2 Work travels: These include travels to and from your job and other official journeys. Time must be allocated to cover distance from the place of residence of a scholar to the place of work and back. The scholar is expected to embark on a number of official trips for conferences/seminars (local and international), conduct of oral examinations (viva voce), moderation of examination questions papers and scripts, some professional associations meetings, etc.

Reasonableness should be exercised in allocating time to these travels and in the choice of means of transportation. In time management, travelling by air is cheaper than travelling by road, if the scholar can afford it! The concern is more on saving time than in saving money.

6.3.3 Personal life: This includes attending to personal hygiene, grooming, meal times, etc. The scholar has to brush teeth, visit the restroom, and shower at least once a day. He/she has to dress up before going to work or to any public event. There must be proper arrangement for each of the three square meals that he/she could afford to take. All these require reasonable allocation of time to accomplish, and the scholar must be ready to sacrifice some of his/her precious time for all these personal life activities.

The question is how reasonable is a scholar in allocating time for these and similar activities? If a scholar allocates more than 30 minutes to shower, or more than 20 minutes to visit the restroom, or more than 10 minutes to comb, or about an hour on dining table eating and chatting, or more than 15 minutes dressing up, then something is wrong with that person's time management process. There is the urgent need for cutting down the allocated time to a reasonable level so that much time savings could be made to allow room for more productive scholarly activities.

6.3.4. Leisure travel: This is about the journey one makes for domestic and leisure reasons. Excursion, visit to museums, zoological gardens, games reserves, tourism sites, etc, are means of recreation and they are stress relieving activities. Such journeys could be made locally or abroad, if the scholar can afford it. Some scholars make annual monetary savings for these types of journeys to be embarked upon during their annual leave period. It is important for the scholar to spend his/her annual leave period and the monetary allowance supporting it wisely.

But care should be exercised as time is spent for these types of journeys; anything that would constitute time wastage must be avoided. Again, if the journey has no economic, social or health benefit it should be scrapped in the future so as to save the time allocated to it in the previous period.

6.3.5 Domestic responsibilities: These are responsibilities like gardening, shopping, housework, etc. Many scholars derive pleasure doing domestic works themselves (including taking care of the domestic needs of their children) instead of employing maids/house helps to take care of such responsibilities. Some scholars carry out various household chores; preparing meals, attending to the garden, go for shopping and etc. All these activities require allocation of substantial time, some demand hours of the scholar's time!

To save time, there is the need for a change of policy/attitude from taking care of most or all of the responsibilities by one self to outsourcing them to some reliable house helps. This would save a lot of time for the scholar to use in facing the challenges of scholarship, more productively.

6.3.6. Official Work/Responsibility: This sub-divides into two main groups:

a. Positive active tasks: These are planned and organised responsibilities. To the scholar, they come in the form of research, teaching, conduct of examination, marking, seminars/conference, publication, etc.

b. Reactive tasks: These are reaction to situations. To the scholar, they come in the form of administrative responsibilities and community services.

These are duties/responsibilities of the scholar detailed out in Chapter 2. Efforts must be made to ensure that, as time is allocated to them, the principle of reasonableness is exercised so that saving could be made of sufficient time after taking care of them satisfactorily. The time saved could be used to cover other contenders to the scholar's time!

6.3.7 Having Leisure/Hobbies: Scholars have their leisure through watching TV, playing/watching football, going out, socialising, etc. A very serious scholar has at least one programme to watch the television for, besides the local and international news. The scholar might be a football, basketball, volleyball, cricket, athletics, golf, etc, fan and would want to watch matches on his/her chosen sport played on the TV or watch it physically in the field of play. The scholar could also be movies lover, cookery lover, drama lover, etc and would want to watch TV station providing any of these leisure services. Time, time, time is needed for all these!

What about the need to socialize with members of the scholar's household, friends/associates, members of the local community, etc in social functions, meetings and get-togethers? All these are needed as part of continuous existence of the scholar as a social being, and time must be accounted for all such interesting activities.

There is, however, the need for caution to be exercised on time allocation to these leisure making activities. Any of the activities that are against the principles (moral, professional or societal) of the scholar, should not be allocated a second of the scholar's time. Reasonable time should be allocated to any of the leisure activity acceptable to a scholar.

It is a mark of poor time consciousness to see a person watching all the programmes on a TV station for up to two hours at a stretch, or watching all the football matches shown during the FIFA World Cup championship or any other major (or even minor) competition for about 5 hours in a day, at a stretch! Not all the matches should be taken as important to that person, if he/she is to be accepted as a good time manager.

The scholar is not expected to waste time in the course of having leisure for refreshment from stress, tiredness and mental fatigue. Reasonableness principle should be exercised in allocating time to leisure activities.

6.4 Providing Rational to What You Do

After determining how much time is spent on each category of activities, there is the need for the time managing scholar to provide answers to the rationale of what he/she does. The scholar should ask the following questions:

1. What do I do that is necessary?

If there are things that were done in the course of the day, week, month or year that are not necessary, then the scholar should conclude that he/she has wasted time doing those things. They should be spotted for avoidance in the next day, week, month or year, thereby saving time to be used for more productive scholarly activities or important leisure activities.

2. What do I do that my subordinate can do better (more economically or more effectively)?

If the scholar is in the position of authority to use subordinate colleagues or students as their mentor, he/she should adopt the management principles of delegation as it promotes training of younger officers, scholars and others to grow. This is especially so if the subordinates have the skills or talent to discharge the responsibilities more economically and more effectively than the superior officer or mentor.

Again, as delegation is done successfully, of the responsibilities to be discharged by the scholar, it would amount to multiplication of the time of the scholar, since it would result to great time saving for him/her. Delegation is the only way through which a good time manager could claim to have been increasing his time beyond the limit of 24 hours, 7 days, and 12 months in a day, week and year!

3. On which things do I spend too much time? Are they worth that much of the time?

After the time audit, the auditor (time manager, as the scholar) should query those activities that enjoy too much time in the course of the day under audit. Are they actually worth that much of the time? If they don't deserve the whole of the time or the quantity of time allocated to them, the auditor has to resolve against repetition of that allocation in the following day.

Time allocation should be strictly based on importance and urgency of activities.

4. Where can I make my most important savings?

The auditor should be concerned about how to make reasonable savings from his/her time allocation to activities. He/she should be critical in scrutinising all the activities that enjoyed the 24 hours of the past day with a view to identifying areas of small and big savings. The most important saving is the total time that could be saved by cutting off unnecessary allocations to some activities and by scrapping unnecessary activities in the budget for the time usage of the next day.

5. How can I avoid taking too much of other people's time?

The scholar, as a good time manager, would not want unexpected visitors to come to his/her home or office to "steal" his/her time. As expected visitors come, they are expected to transact the business on which they are given permission to come and take their leave. This is with a view to allowing the scholar to have ample time for discharging his/her responsibilities.

In the same vein, the scholar should also not have the mentality of taking too much of other people's time. He/she should be a good visitor, a straight-to-the- point discussant of issues while on visit to someone, and a sympathiser of other people as prospective time managers.

6. On what do I spend too little time?

As the auditor checks the activities that consumed his/her time in the past day, some activities might be noted to have been allocated too little time. The question is: is it because they are less important or they are not important at all?

If they are important activities, or more important than those allocated too much time, then there would be the need for reversal of the quantity allocation, in favor of these activities in the next day, week, month or year. But where they are found to be of no importance at all, then the little time allocated to them should be withdrawn and, so, they should be completely eliminated from the budget of next period. Again, time allocation to activities should be strictly based on importance and urgency.

7. What are the causes of my time problems?

This question usually arises when a first-timer time auditor discovers that he/she has a lot of problems with time management and he/she is finding it difficult to explain why the problems persist.

It is always advisable for such a person, especially if he/she is a scholar, to consult an expert in time management for guidance and counseling. There are individual differences to be considered as different people are rendered guidance and counseling services on time management. But many or most of the problems are universal!

8. How can I organize more effectively?

In Chapter 3 we have learnt about how the scholar should be a very good time organiser. When one is able to organise his/her time, it could just be concluded that the person is organising his "person"! So, the best way to organise yourself effectively is to organise your time effectively.

Again, it is advisable to consult experts if time organising is found to be difficult to the scholar. Through appropriate guidance and counseling to be obtained from time management experts, one could become an effective organiser of time and person.

The above self-assessment questionnaire (with 8 items) should assist the time managing scholar to exercise greater control over him-or herself and over all activities being undertaken for the achievement of the desired result and for ensuring self-control and self-discipline.

CHAPTER SEVEN

TIME STEALERS TO THE SCHOLAR

Time wasting activities steal time. They should be spotted and stopped immediately by the scholar for him/her to be accepted as a good time manager. Here are suggested solutions to some common time stealers in the academic system:

7.1 Poor Meeting Objectives

S/N	Cause	Solution
i.	Purpose of the meeting not clearly stated or not clearly made known.	A good time manger would insist on having a clearly drawn up agenda for any meeting, even if it is a family meeting.
ii.	Wrong participants; membership for attendance not clearly defined.	Only invite those who are qualified, that is, relevant members to the meeting.
iii.	Too many meetings; purposeless meetings (may be just to earn sitting allowance and other goodies!)	Review the result in relation to time spent. Is the meeting necessary? If a meeting is not justifiable, it should not be attended.
iv	Poorly conducted meeting or written minutes not prepared.	Appoint a secretary to write action lists (minutes) as accurately as possible.
v.	Irrelevant discussions by some participants at the meeting.	Effective chairmanship is needed, to direct and control the proceedings and ensure orderliness.
vi.	No conclusion or definite time for the meeting to come to an end.	Agenda must state issues to deliberate on and the time for adjournment, even if all issues listed have not been treated by the specified concluding time.
vii.	Too many interruptions from within or without the venue of the meeting.	Ban them (except for fire or riot). This is the responsibility of the Chairman!

Notes:

1. The scholar might have to attend too many meetings in the academic environment alone. He/she is expected to show seriousness as these meetings are conducted so that he/she could insist on the meetings to be as productive as possible. The scholar should not allow meetings to consume his/her time unnecessarily and he/she should guide other participants on the best way to conduct productive meetings.

2. The discipline to be shown on meeting attendance and conduct as highlighted above is applicable to all meetings that might be convened outside the academic environment. The scholar's role remains the same once the meetings are convened.

3. Many experts in time management would advice that a serious person, like the scholar, should always ask two questions on any meeting to be attended: (1) Is the meeting necessary? (2) Is my attendance necessary for the meeting? Any meeting that could be justifiably declared unnecessary should not be attended by the scholar; it would amount to time wastage. The scholar should tactfully avoid (completely or partially) any meeting to which his/her attendance would not add any value, especially if his/her attention is much needed on other pressing issues during the period of the meeting.

7.2 Telephone Interruptions

S/N	Cause	Solution
i.	Conversation too long, no matter who the caller is.	1). Separate chat from information irrespective of who made the call. 2). Discourage unnecessary talk so as to show consciousness to your time management. 3). The scholar, as a good time manager, would not purposelessly engage in making phone calls.
ii.	Rambling conversation, or "beating about the bush".	Plan and list topics to be discussed and go straight to the point. If the call was initiated by you, try to control the conversation to save both parties' time.

Notes:

1. Telephone conversations through calls, text messages and internet browsing do take a lot people's time, scholars are no exception. It is advisable to exercise caution. The scholar, as a good time manager, is not expected to engage in lengthy conversation or encourage anyone else to do that with him/her. He/she is expected to go straight to the point.
2. There is a need for scholars to remind their family members, students and others under their control on the need to avoid misusing their phones on things that are not necessary. It has gone to the extent that students are fond of playing with their phones, conversing/chatting with it or just browsing the internet through it when lectures are going on in the class. A serious teacher would not tolerate such behavior arising from the students in his/her class.

7.3 Lack of Priority

S/N	Cause	Solution
i.	Don't know how to set priority?	Use the organisational system and consult experts on time or resource management.
ii.	Lack time to plan?	Plan time to have time for all your key activities/responsibilities and others!
iii.	Lack self-discipline?	Establish key areas of your day-to-day activities, schedule the activities with sense of reasonableness in time allocation, and monitor progress.
iv	Rather move/act than think?	Always think before you move/act. This ensures effective time utilisation and time saving.

Notes:

1. Priority setting is a principle that is known among scholars all over the world, and this is a fact from the beginning of civilisation. Scholars are expected to be very focus, forward looking and well organised. It is unfortunate if the scholar would give any sign of poor priority setting, which is a clear source of time wastage.

2. As indicated above, the scholar should learn to always think before acting; should invest time to have/save time; and should demonstrate the culture of discipline and sense of responsibility and maturity.

7.4 Not Finishing Assignment

S/N	Cause	Solution
i.	Lack of time limit for an assignment to be completed or a project to be executed.	Set deadlines for yourself and work towards meeting the deadlines. Serious academic institutions normally set deadlines for any assignment given to their staff, and these deadlines should be met by the serious scholar.
ii.	Allowing too many interruptions: unwanted visitors, unnecessary social activities, unproductive discussion physically or over the phone, unnecessary internet browsing, etc.	Set quiet hours to concentrate on accomplishing serious tasks. Ban all time wasting interruptions, as much as possible.
iii.	No overall perspective? You are not focused enough to achieving your goals/objectives in life?	Think about yourself and your job all the time, as you think about other people that you deal with. Your overall perspective should be about how you could use your time to achieve organisational and personal objectives. These objectives should be as ethical as possible.
iv	Too much to do. You cannot do all at a time!	Drop old responsibilities, especially accomplished ones, before taking new responsibilities at any given time. This requires priority setting and queuing up of activities/responsibilities for discharge.

Notes:

1. A good time manager should always make effort to finish assignments no matter how difficult or demanding it is, by or before the deadline set. The scholar, as a good time manager, would not

accept any assignment without deadline or project without lifespan. He/she would make effort to meet the deadline, with all sense of seriousness and respect for the system.

2. Whatever work or activity to be assigned to the students, by the scholar, he/she would want to set deadline for its accomplishment so that he meets the deadline given by the authorities for submission of final results on students' performance. In his/her dealing with students, many assignments are given to the students and deadlines for submission should be fixed as a way of training them to be good time managers in the future.

3. Just as the scholar would not want his/her time to be robbed due to inability to finish assignment/s in good time, he/she should not allow the students to be victims of that circumstance!

7.5 Lack of Self- discipline

S/N	Cause	Solution
i.	Lack of system or principle.	Organise yourself and be a man/woman of principle in whatever you do and in the face of any challenge.
ii.	Forgetfulness.	Write notes on all promises made, all appointments given and all plans/budgets designed for effective utilisation of your time.
iii.	Failure to delegate (duties that could be effectively delegated).	Learn to delegate (to capable subordinates) for training/grooming the young ones and for time saving.
iv	Indecision or confusion.	70% of the tasks on your hand could be handled at once. Try to accomplish what could be done at a specified time and put those tasks behind you. You are then ready to face the tasks ahead!

Note:

1. Self-discipline, which entails self-respect, is what would attract genuine respect to the scholar from his/her colleagues, students and even the authorities in the school, college or university. If the scholar

is not principled in his/her dealing with others; is too forgetful; is unorganised; is indecisive; or self-centered, he/she should not expect honest/genuine respect from those at the top, from contemporaries, from subordinates or even from students. He/she might only be feared since he/she has something to determine on the subordinates or students!

2. The scholar should be a shining example of a person with self-respect and a person that believes in the principle of delegation. He/she should be seen as both a mentor and role model when it comes to the issues of self-discipline and self-respect. He/she should not allow his/her time to be robbed by poor self-discipline, at all.

CHAPTER EIGHT

HOW SCHOLARS GENERALLY WASTE THEIR TIME

To determine how the scholar wastes his/her time, the scholar should just spend some few minutes to sincerely respond to the statements under each of the following identified time wasters, with a simple 'Yes" or "No" answer. A 'yes' suggests a poor time manager, while a 'no' suggests a good time manager. The scholar is to respond to the statements to self and not to any other examiner, meaning that there should be no fear of failure or any embarrassment as the statements are responded to!

8.1 Delay in Taking Action

I delay taking action

Delay in taking action by the scholar is an indication of poor time management; it is a show of inability to discharge responsibilities at the specified time or to meet obligations, including promises made. In other words, the scholar must have directed his/her attention to other non-related matters to cause the delay in taking action on important related matters to his/her responsibilities.

Taking action and making decision are related, but they are not the same. Making decision might need more time for scrutiny than taking action. Taking action could be keeping something in view (KIV) until later time, while making decision is a final position on an issue, which at times demands some consultations.

For the scholar, he/she is expected to take immediate action on conducting his/her classes for students, submission of questions paper and marking scheme at due time, submission of examination results at due time, submission of paper for presentation at a conference or publication in a journal, etc. Delay in taking these kind of actions beyond the stipulated time suggests that the scholar is not a good time manager. The delay by the bad time manager might affect the organisational system as a whole.

So, if the scholar's response to the above statement is 'yes' it means that the scholar is a time waster, a poor time manager!

8.2 Spending Little Time on Planning

I don't spent enough time on planning

In the discipline of management, planning is unavoidable, as the saying goes: if you fail to plan, you are planning to fail! Planning is the beginning of management, as all other functions of management depends on its quality.

The scholar, as a good time manager, has to spend enough time on planning, since everything he/she does demands some degree of prior planning before organising resources for accomplishment, directing an affair and ensuring effective control of all the activities necessary for the achievement of the desired goals/objectives.

So, if the scholar's response to the above statement is 'yes', then it means that the scholar is not a good time manager; he/she is a time waster!

8.3 Failure to Delegate

I tend to do things myself instead of delegating

The management principle of delegation promotes the culture of 'grooming' or 'mentoring' young officers to become senior officers in the future, and it allows senior officers to relieve themselves of responsibilities that could be effectively discharged by the young officers in training. So, delegation allows the time manager the opportunity to save more time which could be used for other productive activities. As stated in Chapter 5, good time managers increase their time beyond the apparent limitation through delegation!

For the scholar to say that he/she does not delegate responsibility is enough for one to conclude that the scholar is not a good time manager, specifically, and that he/she is not a reliable manager, generally! So, the correct response to the statement above is 'no', if the scholar is actually a good time manager.

8.4 Failure to Prioritise

I don't prioritise

Any scholar that does not prioritise his/her activities is not only a bad time manager but an unserious person! With many competing activities to perform, the scholar has to always set priority lines as the activities are taken care of one after the other. This priority setting is dependent on the scholar's ability to appreciate the degree of importance or necessity of the responsibilities to be discharged at any given point in time.

So, a scholar, as a good time manager, should give a 'no' response to this statement. It would be very upsetting to hear any scholar giving a 'yes' answer to the statement!

8.5 Wasting Too Much Time in Meetings

I waste a lot of time in meetings

In the academic community, especially university community, a lot of meetings are held, especially as many committees exist for the discharge of many responsibilities in the course of running the affairs of the community. The scholar might belong to some university committees, college/faculty/school committees and departmental committees. In the larger society, he/she might belong to some federal, state or local government committees. He/she could also belong to some local/social community committees. All these would require attendance of meetings physically or through a proxy, in some few cases.

But when a scholar attends a meeting, he/she is expected to be adequately convinced that the meeting is necessary (especially if it is based on previous meeting minutes); that its agenda is clearly spelt out; that it is well organised and chaired by a serious person; and that there is definite/maximum time for the meeting to be adjourned. These are issues to be considered by the serious scholar to make sure that he/she does not waste unnecessary time in meetings, bearing in mind his/her time budget for the day that covers many other responsibilities apart from the meeting(s).

The scholar who is considerate on meeting attendance and administration as described above is in a good position to answer

71

'no' to the statement above. Otherwise, the response should be 'yes', which signifies poor time management.

8.6 Allowing Visitors to Stay Too Long

Too many visitors stay too long or are unexpected

As a scholar you cannot avoid visitors coming to your office or home, with or without appointment. When they come, some may wish to engage you in gossips on the situation in your school or on the campus; engage you in national political discourse; engage you in happening in sports arena (if you are sports fan), etc. Many of them, if allowed, might not want to take their leave immediately after transacting the real purpose and intent of their visit in the first place.

The scholar, as a good time manager, should discourage this kind of attitude, diplomatically or bluntly. But many scholars are finding it difficult to come into terms with such visitors.

The scholar is expected to adapt a very good policy for receiving and entertaining visitors at home and in the office, with a sense of respect, straight-forwardness and prudence in time utilisation for the visits and for other competing activities/responsibilities.

The response to the above statement should be 'no', but in reality it is 'yes' to many scholars. This suggests poor time management from the scholars concerned. In fact, some scholars appear like gossip-mongers waiting for gossipers to come to their offices or homes at any given period with the latest gossips peddling around.

8.7 Working with Poorly Trained Subordinates

My subordinates are not trained enough

If subordinates are not well trained, they should not be seen as materials for delegation of responsibilities; they can't discharge the responsibilities satisfactorily. The training at school/university should be enough for subordinates to be utilised as they are assigned delegated responsibilities. But many educational institutions (up to university level) provide sub-standard training to their students. For this reason, there is need for training and re-training of subordinates so that they catch up with the system in place and the standard set for successful operations.

72

The response of the scholar, as a good time manager, to the above statement should be 'no', since his/her subordinates should have been well trained enough. Where the response is 'yes' it means that the scholar is not managing his time well, and that he has no much concern for the growth and development of his/her subordinates.

8.8 Failure to Say 'No'

I don't say 'NO' often enough

The scholar, as a good time manager, is not expected to be a yes-man/woman! He/she should be ready to say 'No' to some requests, especially those bordering on appointments which would affect his/her time management process. He/she should always pass judgment on request for his/her time based on availability of the time.

When the scholar commits self to a function/event he/she should not promise the same time to any other function/event organisers. For example, when the scholar promises to attend a farewell party of a transferring colleague by 8pm, he/she should not accept another invitation for any other event at the same time or close to that time (example at 7.30pm, 9 pm, etc). He/she should decline the invitation as diplomatically and politely as possible. Alternatively, he/she should cancel the first appointment giving satisfactory apologies to the organisers in good time.

Not only on time utilisation specifically, on any other activity in life, the scholar should know his/her limitations and respond to request or even directive with the answer 'no' if he/she knows that it would not be possible to do what is requested. Care might have to be taken in saying 'no' to superior officers, as some of them would not take it lightly even if they know that the capacity to do what they require of the subordinate is not there. What they expect is that the subordinate should try his/her best first before they accept that he/she can't do what is required of him/her!

In the military formation, they go by the slogan: "obey before complain" and, so, they don't tolerate the word 'no' coming from a junior officer who is required to discharge a responsibility. This suggests that in a militarised environment, the scholar has to be careful in using the word 'no' to show his/her limitation as a good time manager!

So, the appropriate response to the statement above is the bitter 'no', otherwise it would suggest that the scholar is not a good time manager. But caution should be exercised in giving that response where it is not acceptable.

8.9 Being a Fire-Fighter Instead of Fire-Preventer

I spent too much time fire-fighting instead of preventing troubles

Fire outbreak is mainly caused by carelessness, resulting from poor planning of activities. If one does not plan well, his/her ability to organise and control trouble is suspected and in the end he/she would resort to fighting preventable fire! As mentioned earlier, if you fail to plan, you are actually planning to fail!

The scholar, as a good time manager, is a preventer of trouble (which takes less time) rather than a fighter of trouble (which takes much time). So, his/her response to the above statement should be 'no'. A 'yes' answer suggests acceptance of troubleshooting as a time waster.

8.10 Acting without Thinking

I don't have enough time for thinking

The system of thought is expected to be applied on whatever the scholar does. The good scholar is naturally a thinker, ultimately a philosopher! Adequate and sufficient time is expected to be allocated, by the good scholar, for thinking before taking any action in the course of discharging his/her responsibilities.

So, the scholar, as a good time manager, is expected to give a 'no' answer to the above statement, otherwise he/she should be seen as a time waster, a poor time manager. A scholar should always have enough time for thinking!

8.11 Allowing 'Communication Gap' to Exist

Breakdown in communication takes up a lot of my time

Communication gap is the cause of most organisational problems, from the family level to corporate level up to governmental level. The scholar is a good communicator, who would not allow communication gap to exist in his/her relationship with colleagues (senior or junior), students, and others that have some businesses to transact with him/her in the course of discharging his numerous responsibilities.

When breakdown in communication occurs, controlling the damage would take up a lot of time making good of the damage controller(s). Therefore, it is always better to prevent it than to make any effort at remedying its consequences.

The scholar, as a good time manager, would provide a 'no' response to the above statement, since he is not expected to allow the breakdown in communication to happen in the first place for it to take a lot of his/her time. When it happens, it has to be accepted as a time waster to the scholar concerned!

8.12 Failure to Meet Deadlines

I fall behind on deadlines too often

Falling behind on deadlines is a mark of inefficiency and ineffectiveness. Deadlines for completion of classes/lectures, for submission of examination questions and marking schemes, marked scripts of students and final result sheets, etc are normally set by the relevant authorities in the school, college or university system for the system to work well. If the scholar could not meet with these deadlines, it means that he/she does not fit into the system. The deadlines could also be on submission of abstract and, later, full paper for conference presentation or publication, and other deadlines known in the academic cycle.

The scholar that fails behind a deadline is a big disappointment to academic system and to scholarship as a whole. Apparently, that person is to be tagged as a poor time manager or a time waster!

The scholar, as a good time manager, is expected to give a quick 'no' response to the above statement. Those scholars that should sincerely give a ''yes' response to this statement need to re-examine themselves and their conscience in view of the fact that they are really doing a lot of damages to the educational system that employs them.

8.13 Misappropriation of Time

I don't have enough time to spend

Time is equally endowed! Nobody is short-changed on time endowment/allocation. Time adequacy and sufficiency to mankind is a matter of planning, organising, directing and controlling of the limited time. When one manages the time well and prioritises activities/responsibilities well, time to spend is bound to be enough!

The scholar, as a good time manager, is not expected to join the "complain game" about adequacy of time to spend; he/she is expected to go by the principle of "living within your means" in spending his/her time in taking care of the scholarship responsibilities and other domestic and personal activities of the day, week, month or year.

So, the scholar, as a good time manager, should give a 'no' response to the above statement, as a 'yes' response suggests ungratefulness on the time endowed to him/her by God for effective utilisation!

8.14 "Too Many Things" To Do

I have too many things to do

Having many things to do is appropriate, but having "too" many things to do is a mark of poor time management, which should not be emphasized by a serious scholar.

The scholar, as a good time manager, should always have reasonable number of things to do at any given time. He/she is not expected to carry "too many things" that could not be taken care of within the limited time, especially as unimportant and not urgent things are inclusive. The principle of priority setting is to be brought to bear.

So, the correct response to the above statement is 'no', otherwise the scholar is to be seen as a poor time manager - a time waster!

CHAPTER NINE

OBSERVING TIME MANAGEMENT MATRIX

9.1 Key Terms of Time Management Matrix

Importance and Urgency are two key terms emphasised by Stephen R. Covey in his book titled: **"The Seven Habits of Highly Effective People"**. The two terms are emphasised in the book as instruments of prioritisation of activities by highly effective people. Everything important and everything urgent should be seen as a matter of necessity in the time management process of a serious person, especially the scholar.

Covey was an American educator, author, businessman, and keynote speaker who lived in this world for 80 years (1932 – 2012). Apart from **"The Seven Habits of Highly Effective People"**, which is his most popular book (more than 25 million copies of it were produced and sold), his other books include: First Things First, Principle-Centered Leadership, The Seven Habits of Highly Effective Families, The Eighth Habit, The Leader In Me, How Schools and Parents Around the World Are Inspiring Greatness, and One Child at a Time. He was a professor at the Jon Huntsman School of Business at Utah State University at the time of his death (July 16, 2012).

Covey was one of the most influential and motivational speakers in the field of management science the world has ever witnessed. He thought of the terms 'importance' and 'urgency' while developing his popular time management grid or matrix, which is enjoying worldwide acceptance and further studies by scholars and professionals in management science.

The two terms are the determining factors on the quantity of time the scholar is to allocate to his/her flood of responsibilities or activities, which are necessary for him/her to do excellent work in his/her chosen career, while at the same time enjoying peace of mind. Every activity or responsibility is to be weighted in the scale of importance and urgency before deciding on the time to be allocated to it.

Importance, significance or relevance is about the benefit derivable from an activity, function or responsibility by the scholar, his/her organisation or both, as the activity is discharged within the time available to the particular scholar. Although activities or responsibilities have different levels of importance/significance, every activity must have a justifiable reason for its discharge. If importance could not be established on an activity, no time should be allocated to it!

The scholar has a flood of activities or responsibilities to perform, as discussed in Chapter 3. It is for him/her to decide on the importance of those identified activities to his/her professional development, their necessity towards achieving the organisational objectives or their importance in adding value to the immediate or larger community within which the scholar lives. If an activity has no value to any of the issues raised here, it should be declared unimportant and, so, it should be allocated zero or very little time by the scholar.

The term urgency is no longer reserved for special occasion; it is used as an everyday occurrence. It is any occurrence that demands immediate attention of the performer of an activity or responsibility. It normally goes with meeting deadline, which could be for anytime related to a minute, an hour, a week, a month, a year, a decade, etc. If urgent responsibilities are not discharged at the due time, the failure might create some devastating negative effects on the scholar, his/her organisation or both.

Covey combined the two wonderful terms, together with their opposites ('not important' and 'not urgent'), to come up with the beautiful matrix/grid, which is described below and then reasonably discussed.

Covey's Time Management Matrix

	Urgent	Not urgent
Important	Quadrant 1 • Crises • Emergencies • Pressing problems • Deadline - driven projects	Quadrant 2 • Planning • Prevention • Relationship building • Recognising new opportunities • Recreation
Not Important	Quadrant 3 • Interruptions, some calls • Some mail, some reports • Some meetings • Proximate, pressing matters • Popular activities	Quadrant 4 • Trivia, busy work • Some mail • Some phone calls • Pleasant activities **TIME WASTERS!**

According to Covey, Quadrant I is for the immediate and important deadlines; Quadrant II is for long-term strategising and development; Quadrant III is for time pressured distractions; and Quadrant IV is for trivial issues/matters, which are declared as **time wasters**. We discuss these four quadrants one-by-one:

9.2 Urgent and Important

Activities or responsibilities in this Quadrant need immediate attention and they should enjoy top priority setting in the scholar's time budget. The scholar should be quick at solving crisis at the infancy level before it matures to become uncontrollable; he/she should pay attention to any dimension of emergencies (personal, official or social); he/she should take enough time to solve pressing problems that are under his/her control and capability; and should accomplish all projects meant for his/her execution in line with the given deadlines.

Looking at the specific responsibilities of the scholar, class teaching (of undergraduate and postgraduate students as per the lecture timetable for an academic semester or session); conduct of continuous assessment of students' performance; submission of questions paper, marking scheme and other required documents within the established deadline; submission of marked scripts and result sheet on the performance of the students within the deadline; submission of abstract of a paper for conference or a full paper for publication in a journal/book of readings;

79

submission of report on an assignment given by the school, college or university authorities; are examples of responsibilities/activities that are to be rated as Quadrant 1 items. These activities are urgent and important for the scholar to take care of as efficiently and effectively as possible.

Again, the scholar might be saddled with administrative responsibility like level/ programme coordinator, head of section/department, dean of a school/faculty, principal, rector, provost, vice chancellor, etc. He/she is bound to encounter a lot of Quadrant 1 activities, which he/she is expected to discharge with all sense of responsibility, maturity, morality, and humility within the available time.

Undermining these Quadrant 1 activities is unacceptable in a serious educational institution or research institute. It is highly unethical for the scholar to throw away these activities for other activities that is not relevant to his/her personal development or the development of the students put under his/her care. Discharging these responsibilities and meeting the deadlines set in the process are the main reasons why a "perceived scholar" is employed into the academic system. Failure to be effective and efficient in the discharge of the Quadrant 1 responsibilities suggests that the person involved does not reflect the attributes of a serious scholar.

9.3 Not Urgent but Important

The activities or responsibilities in Quadrant 2 have no sense of immediacy, but must be done. They include planning of activities, prevention of unnecessary distractions, relationship building, recognising new opportunities and recreation.

We have learnt in Chapter 4 that planning is the beginning of effective management. Where planning and its components (like budget, forecasting, estimation, standard-setting, etc) are weak or absent, effectiveness would never be there. Preventive measures need to be taken against all anticipated unfavorable events (risks), to emphasise on the maxim that 'prevention is better than cure" or that it is better to 'be a fire-preventer than a fire-fighter'. The scholar should be a good relationship builder, for him-or herself and for the organisation where he/she works. Time is also needed to create and recognise opportunities for advancement and to plan as to how to utilise the opportunities. There is also the need for reasonable allocation of time for recreational activities so as to keep fit all the time.

Looking at the responsibilities of the scholar, there is the need for importance to be attached to adequate planning before entering any class of students for teaching, showing creativity as original questions are set for the semester examination, conduct of continuous assessment (CA) on students' performance to determine and make available their CA or carrying marks in good time, marking students' examination scripts as fairly as possible, beating all the deadlines on teaching responsibilities and those of conference attendance and paper submission for publication, report write up and submission, etc.

The scholar is expected to be a good preventer of trouble, crisis and other risky situations rather than being a problem solver in the system. He/she is expected to plan time for building relationship with the outside world so that he/she could market him-or herself and the institution to which he/she belongs, and, sometimes, even his/her country as a whole. The scholar needs time for exercising the body system/recreation, so as to remain healthy and active.

Again, scholars holding positions of administrative responsibilities within the system are expected to be shining examples on effective and productive planning, initiative and creative prevention measures against distractions, effective relationship building with the outside world, opportunity creation and many more strategic management measures, as they administer the affairs of the academic environment (school, college, research center or university). Time must be voted for all these.

Quadrant 2 is like the think-tank of time management; the engine room for empowering the scholar with productive and goal-scoring ideas. The Quadrant is not about what to be done urgently, but about the activities to be done in the immediate and distant future. In order words, the quality of the result to be obtained from the activities in each of the other Quadrants, especially Quadrant 1, is dependent on the quality of Quadrant 2 activities. The scholar, as a good time manager, should be very mindful of the necessity of the activities relevant to this Quadrant.

9.4 Urgent but not Important

The activities in Quadrant 3 are not tied to a person's priorities, but they involve other people's urgencies. They are not important to the scholar because they are not tied to his/her priorities in life. But since he/she cares for humanity, he/she might wish to take care of them so that the urgency in them, in the contemplation of the people he/she cares for, could be satisfied.

Example of Quadrant 3 activities include: Interruptions (such as some phone calls that are not important to the scholar, but the caller needs an urgent information from him/her); Some mails (including emails), which might not add any value to the scholar, but sent to elicit information from him/her; some meetings (which might not be necessary or might not have clear cut agenda, but "organised" to benefit some people); proximate, pressing matters to other people in the scholar's organisation or local community but have no specific bearing with him/her; popular activities (like FIFA World Cup, Olympic, World Athletics Fiesta, Cultural Fiesta, Trade Fair, etc) which might not add any value to the scholar but imposed on him/her to watch or attend by his/her family members, friends or colleagues.

Looking at the responsibilities of the scholar, the activities in Quadrant 3 are to be allocated some few time; mainly because of the need for him/her to be a very good community activist and "social worker"! He/she needs to incorporate his/her participation in the community projects and concern for individual members of the community into his/her time budget. So, although the activities here are mainly influenced by others, the scholar should accord some respect to them by sparing some few time for them since he/she urgently needs to take care of those activities in order to please relations, friends, colleagues and associates.

In any case, the activities in this Quadrant should never be prioritised over the activities in Quadrant 1 and 2; they are to be allocated some "occasional" few times that might not harm the more serious activities identified in the first two Quadrants.

9.5 Not important and not urgent

The activities in Quadrant 4 are **time wasters** to any time user, especially to the serious scholar. They deserve zero or very little time from the scholar. Examples of these activities are: trivial (non-value-adding or "busy work" activity); junk or spam mails and e-mails, some phone calls; unproductive pleasant activities; etc. These activities only consume the scholar's time without adding any good knowledge or experience to his/her person or organisation.

82

The scholar is not expected to engage him-or herself in any trivial activity that would show that he/she is "busy" whereas he/she is not producing anything good for humanity. Junk mails or emails, when recognised as such, should be deleted to the trash immediately (the seconds involved in doing that is the only time they deserve)! Any phone call that is realised to be useless (examples are calls from phone scammers, persons known to be nuisance or time wasters, etc) should not be listened to, but diplomacy should be shown in declining them.

Unproductive pleasant activities are those activities that might not have any positive impact in the life of a person, his/her organisation or the society as a whole. Examples of these activities are committing valuable time to watching immoral movies (morality here is a relative term for each person to accord his/her definition), taking valuable time to read useless novels (this is also dependent on what is useful or useless to the reader), involvement in sinful activities as a means of deriving pleasure (this is also dependent on the faith of the person involved).

The scholar is expected to assess him - or herself before deciding on the actions to be taken on all the activities relevant to Quadrant 4. Once an activity is declared not important and not urgent to the needs of his/her organisation, and to the benefit of the larger community, the only time the activity deserves is the length of time it would take the scholar to delete, drop, cancel, or block it completely!

9.6 Proposed Percentage Time Allocation to the 4 Quadrants

Covey, the inventor of the time management matrix, says that many people spend most of their time in Quadrant 4 and almost no time in Quadrant 2. This conclusion was drawn from his many years of studies on time management, consultation with managers of various public and private sector organisations, and conduct of seminars and workshops to wide variety of people across the world. When many people spend most of their time on activities that are not important and not urgent to themselves and their organisations, there would be no hope at all for the achievement of the set objectives of the organisations and those of the economies in which they operate.

This is a clear explanation on the reason why most developing economies could not attain the desired level of development, no matter the quantity of the other resources they have, as their public and private sector organisations are managed by very poor time managers who

83

allocate more of their time to Quadrant 4 activities than to Quadrant 1 activities. Again, these managers are found to be careless in allocating appropriate time to Quadrant 2, which is the engine room for effectiveness and efficiency in managing the affairs of any organisation.

In fact, concern on time management appears as if it is an issue for the western world alone, as most people in the southern hemisphere consider time management as a burden to the extent that in Africa, for example, leaders and followers appear to go with the belief that they have their special time, which is called "African Time"! They appear as if they are 'disturbed' with insistence about the need for time management to be institutionalised as it is being practiced in the "west". Both leaders and followers appear not to have the time needed to learn or read about how to manage their time, not to talk of having the time to conduct personal time audit with a view to finding out areas of time saving to be used in favor of more productive activities in the future. What a problem!

The concept of African Time is only signifying that many leaders and followers in the continent of Africa are "time failures", failing to keep to time, to fulfill promises, to meet agreed deadlines, to be conscious of time, to save time and to utilise time effectively to achieve the desired results. Then one wonder as to what is special about this derogatory term? Serious scholars in the continent should avoid presenting themselves in such a way that the term could be used against them!

Going back to the time management matrix and the appropriate time allocation, Covey proposes that to achieve maximum results from what we do, we must complete tasks in Quadrant 1 first, then Quadrant 2, followed by Quadrant 3 and Quadrant 4. Although we should avoid spending time on Quadrant 4 activities, a few times must be allocated to deleting, cancelling, banning or blocking those activities.

It is hereby proposed that the scholar's daily time percentage allocation should be in the region of: 50: 30: 15: 05 for Quadrants 1, 2, 3 and 4, respectively! Each scholar should consider his/her peculiarity in agreeing on the appropriate percentage allocation to make. But can one be sure that no serious scholar would allocate more than 5% of his/her daily time to Quadrant 4 activities?

CHAPTER TEN

GOLDEN GUIDES FOR EXCELLENT TIME MANAGEMENT

The following 20 points serve as golden guides to scholars if they are to manage their time effectively and assure themselves of success in their research, teaching and community service responsibilities:

10.1 Develop Fixed Daily Routine

The scholar should develop a clearly spelt out daily routine and comply with it to the letter. Routine things are to be done at the routine times designed/allocated for them.

Daily routines include tasks carried out to look after personal, family, social, recreational and spiritual needs. These are things that demand the valuable time of the scholar, and if care is not taken they might be unjustifiably marginalised or allocated unnecessary quantity of time.

The scholar has to make it a matter of Quadrant 2 activity to develop the fixed daily routine very well and a matter of Quadrant 1 activity to implement it religiously!

10.2 Do Important Jobs at Fresh Time

The scholar should always allocate his/her best time for important jobs/activities. He/she always does important things when he/she is fresh or at his/her best. Important activities are not to be reserved to a time when he/she is tired or is not in good mood to work.

Looking at the TM grid, Quadrant 1 activities are those to be taken care of fully when the scholar is at his/her best. This would accelerate achievement of personal and organisational goals/objectives in good time.

10.3 Time Budget and Budgetary Control

Like is always the case with financial and other resources, time, as a resource, should be subjected to effective budgeting and budgetary control so as to manage its scarcity adequately. Budget is an aspect of planning, which is a Quadrant 2 activity to be allocated enough time in the life of a scholar. Budget is the most important instrument for managing scarcity of resources, especially time.

A serious scholar would set time limit for all the identified important activities of the day, week, month or year and stick to the budget made, with a view to exercising control over all the lined up activities. The budgetary control component comes in at the end of the day, week, month or year when the scholar does the time audit to evaluate his/her time management performance in line with the accomplishment made during the previous period so as to plan better against the future period.

Time audit should incorporate variance analysis to be conducted on the differences that are likely to occur between time allocations to activities and the actual times taken on the identified activities. Conclusions are to be reached on the favorableness or non-favorableness of the variances before deciding on the corrective/improvement actions to be taken in the future. Enough time is needed for this exercise of budgeting and budgetary control, which is inclusive of audit, so that a lot of time-savings could be made and clear sense of direction obtained in the course of the life of a scholar.

10.4 Anything Important Must Be Done

The scholar must try to accomplish anything identified as important to his/her life. He/she is not to put off unpleasant or difficult task, if they are also important.

Life challenges come with some obstacles, hurdles and risks. The scholar should know that if efforts are not made to accomplish tasks in line with the obstacles, risks or uncertainties surrounding them, there would be no hope for success in life, and the organisational objectives could not be achieved.

Enough time must be allocated to all tasks that are classified as important, and they have to be taken up squarely for accomplishment, no matter how unpleasant or difficult they are.

10.5 Avoid Interruptions

The scholar needs to be very focused, strategic and progressive so as to move knowledge forward, develop better generation for the future and contribute positively towards achieving the noble objective of sustainable development of the larger community. In the course of facing the challenges for all these, there are obstructions to encounter at one point or another. The scholar should be able to analyse them and take appropriate measures to avoid them.

In time management, all interruptions should be banned during meetings/briefings, class discussions, conference/seminar sessions, data analysis, report write up, and other academic and administrative activities. But analysis should be conducted first to ensure that they are actually interruptions before steps are taken to avoid them.

10.6 Put off Everything that is not Important

As discussed in chapter 9, everything that is declared not important and not urgent (Quadrant 4 activities) should be put off immediately. It should not take a second longer than the time needed to delete, cancel or just ignore it.

It is unfortunate that some experts, like Covey (1990), have discovered that many people spend most of their times on things that are not important to their lives, their organisations and the economy within which they live. This is a very serious problem to humanity, which demands all hands to be on deck to find lasting solution to.

Scholars should be different on this issue; they are not expected to be part of time wasters that engage their precious time on things that are not important to their lives. They should be preaching against time wastage at different forums and they should be acting against it, as a way teaching by doing!

10.7 Publicise Quiet Hour

The scholar should set quite time for concentrated works to be done, for deeper meetings/briefings, for intimacy with family members, etc. He/she needs quite time for interaction with students in the class and sometimes in his/her office room; for meeting with his/her colleagues; for deep-rooted research and report write ups, etc. When the quite time/hour is set, he/she should make visitors understand it and politely requests them to allow him/her to effectively utilise it.

The quite hour setting should also be extended to visitors to his/her home. They should be made to understand when they are not welcome; may be anytime after 9 pm and any time before 8 am. The scholar could also specify days for visit to his/her home or even visit to his/her office and the specific period for the visit. Diplomacy is needed in making

87

relations, friends, colleagues and other associates understand this principle.

In fact serious public and private sector organisations set their visitors' time and publicise it clearly, so that visitors know that the other hours of the day are for their employees to concentrate on their work and produce the required results for the achievement of the organisational goals/objectives.

10.8 Do One Thing at a Time

Chucking up things makes things to be unmanageable; a lot of time might go without achieving anything. Again, the whole system might negatively be affected by this bad attitude to time management.

The scholar should learn to do important things one-by-one, based on the priority setting made on the important things. He/she might have assumed too much things in his/her life, by him-or herself or imposed by circumstances but, when it comes to execution, those things are to be handled one after another. It is then that the whole lot could be accomplished successfully and satisfactorily within the time available.

Where the scholar has power or influence, he/she should make sure that: (I) at a meeting, participants should be talking one-by-one; (ii) when things are distributed, collectors should be collecting onc-by-one; (iii) when people come for inquiry, they are to be listened to one-by-one; (iv) when boarding a vehicle or aeroplane, passengers should be entering one-by-one; and (v) while eating food or drinking water, the swallow should be progressing one-by-one!

10.9 Plan Phone Calls and Stick to the Plan

This issue is part of time budgeting but, because of the influence of phone calls in the knowledge management era, it is hereby taken separately. Phone calls, texting and other phone usages are consuming a lot of time of many scholars, their students, colleagues, friends, relations and associates. Scholars have to be decisive on how they should manage the use of their phones and how they should manage relationship between them and other people through the use of phones. This is where planning how to use phone comes in.

The scholar has to decide the specific time periods to make use of his/her phone, when to switch it off and when to put it in silence or vibration mode. He/she needs to stick to the time period set aside for making calls or sending smses and be very straight to the points while on the calls made to others so as to avoid wasting their time on unnecessary issues.

When the scholar is called by a relation, friend, student, colleague or any associate, he/she should be diplomatic enough to ensure that only important issues are discussed. He/she might go to the extent of "cutting off" the line if it becomes apparent that the caller on the other side could not sense that "time is off" on the issue(s) at stake!

10.10 Where ever Possible, Finish Your Task

The scholar should not believe too much in "tomorrow". What is worth doing today should be accomplished today; one should not be too sure that he/she would see "tomorrow". After all, the "tomorrow" in view would come with its numerous tasks to be accomplished.

So, efforts are to be made to ensure that all tasks for a day are accomplished that day; it gives a high sense of satisfaction to the scholar and it makes him/her very ready to face the challenges of "tomorrow", where it becomes real. "Tomorrow" in this context refers to next day, next week, next month, next year, next decade or next generation.

10.11   Keep Records of Ideas and Appointments

In the course of his/her life activities and interactions with many people, the scholar makes a lot of promises, gives a lot of appointments and generates a lot of ideas. It might be difficult for all these to be remembered up-head, and failure to remember would cause him/her to breach some of the promises made or appointments given, and would make him/her to lose a lot of good ideas that could be used in the process of his/her research, teaching or community service.

To ensure effective management of time and ideas, the scholar should always keep a note book to collect ideas or to note down the appointments given on some activities or promises made to a number of people on some issues. This way he/she would be seen to be well organised and self-disciplined and doing this would win a sincere respect for the scholar from his colleagues, students, relations, friends and others.

The scholar might employ a personal assistant (PA) to help ensure that he/she is well organised and coordinated as a responsible person, by keeping tracks of all his/her engagements and by making sure that

89

he/she is not lost in any of the assumed responsibilities. The PA might also be delegated some responsibilities of the scholar, after due training on how to take care of the responsibilities to be delegated.

10.12 Arrange for Breaks When Ineffective

There is the need for rest: full rest (sleeping) or partial rest (some break times). The scholar should appreciate this fact. All organisations, anywhere in the world, allow times for breaks for their employees. This is to ensure that work is not interrupted due to fatigue, burn-out and illnesses.

The scholar should arrange his/her breaks at times when he/she cannot work effectively. For class teaching, using semester system, each hour of lecture deserves a maximum of 10 minutes for break, giving a total of 30 minutes break time for a 3-credit course per class. For data collection, data analysis and cleansing, data interpretation and report writing, some breaks times are required to allow the brain to get refreshed and the body system to rest. On all dimensions of community service, the scholar is expected to arrange break times as appropriately as possible.

Even though the scholar is expected to work hard and produce reasonable results, he/she is not expected to work harder than his/her capacity. Arranging break times in the course of working hard is a means of enhancing the capacity of the scholar. The moment he/she realizes that he/she is weak or ineffective in the course of discharging any of his/her responsibilities, the best thing for him/her to do is to take a rest: full or partial.

10.13 Learn to Say "No", Where Possible

As mentioned earlier, the scholar is never a "yes" man/woman; saying "no" on what is not dischargeable within the limited time is part of the principle of that person. But the context within which the "no" response is to be given needs to be understood.

When the time manager is a subordinate to a "militarised boss", who always expect obedience to instruction before complaint, the time manager should be careful not to say "no", but just say: 'I will try, sir'! Later frank excuse might be given as to why it was not possible for the instruction to be carried out as required, emphasising on the time factor.

The scholar finds him-or herself in many situations where the "no" response is required, and he/she should learn to offer it, with some degree of politeness and diplomacy. Failure to be principled enough to say "no" in many occasions makes a "perceived scholar" to be a highly disrespectable person, as he/she is seen as a liar, a deceiver, a cheat, unreliable and unethical.

10.14 Do Similar Jobs at a Time

In time management it is time saving to do similar type of jobs at the same time, for examples all phone calls one after another; all selection interviews one candidate after another; all supplies of goods one customer after another, etc. When you create several times for similar work/activity that could be accomplished at the same time, a lot of unnecessary time wastage would be incurred.

Similar types of works/responsibilities of the scholar are to be taken care of at the same time; doing them at different times causes a lot of time wastage, unnecessarily. Marking of students scripts should be done at the same time, not to be scattered over many periods of time; consultations with the students should have a designed time for all the students to consult; data screening or interpretation needs some concentrated time for accomplishment and not many short-short time periods, etc.

The scholar should appreciate this fact to utilise his/her limited time effectively on this note.

10.15 Conduct Time Audit

This golden guide for effective time management has been adequately treated in Chapter 6 of this book and, so, a serious scholar requires no additional talk about it here. He/she is only advised to comply fully with the process prescribed for the conduct of the audit on daily, weekly, monthly and annual basis. The benefits are numerous!

10.16 Only Take Work Home if You Intend To Do It

Some officers at various levels of the organisational structure, in both the public and private sector organisations, are fond of carrying office works that have not been done in the office to home. Some do that only "for show", just to give the impression that they are officers, with too much responsibilities in their organisations, going by the file or brief case they carry home. This is unethical!

Office related works should be done in the office, what could not be accomplished today, after investing all the working hours on it, should be postponed to the next day. It is not for an officer to refuse doing his/her work in the office or to waste the office hours on gossips and other time wasters, and then to complain that there is no time for the work to be done in the office, but at home. Some officers, even as they carry the file (s) to their homes, would not even look at the file (s) until the following day when they would transfer them back to the office again. This is not an encouraging practice to be nurtured.

The scholar is not expected to be a person that carries work home if it is suppose to be done in the office. But, unfortunately, many scholars do many of their works at home: lecture notes development, marking of students' scripts, compilation of continuous assessment/carrying marks and final results, conference/journal articles paper write ups, etc. This attitude shows many scholars are working round the clock; doing scholarly works for 24 hours!

Even though many scholars actually do the works they carry home, it is important that they learn to do only those works that are important and necessary, and that they should not "encroach" into the time meant for their affectionate feelings with their family members while at home.

10.17 Think Then Act

This golden guide for excellent time management is emphasising on the need for a good time manager to always think deeply and seriously before taking any action. Good time management should be demonstrated in both theory and practice, with 'theory' part given by the need for adequate 'thinking', while the 'practice' part is given by the need for sincere 'acting' as a time manager.

The scholar is always a good thinker who is always expected to be guided by the deep thoughts given to issues. In his/her time management process, the principle of thinking before moving/acting is paramount. Anything short of this means that the person in view is not a scholar, but something else!

10.18 Do Things Adequately But Don't Be a Perfectionist

No human is perfect; only God is perfect. This is a general belief to all followers of various religions in the world. So, when somebody is excellent in a particular work or profession, he/she could attempt perfection which is not attainable, since he/she is not God. To reach the level of excellent performance in the discharge of any duty is not a small task, and that performance should only be subjected to efforts at sustenance.

The scholar, while managing his/her time, should make effort to ensure that there is continuous improvement in his/her performance (from fair-good-very good-excellent). When the performance of a scholar, as a good time manager, becomes excellent, then he/she needs to sustain it at that level through continuous effort at reaching perfection!

Even though it is not advisable for the scholar to be a perfectionist, he/she is expected to be a sustainable developer in the discharge of all his/her responsibilities and at all levels. This is possible if he/she does things adequately at those levels, not relenting on the good efforts he/she is known with.

10.19 Always Work With a Resolution

After the conduct of time audit, there is the need for the scholar to adopt a resolution on what to do with his/her time in the next period (hour, day, week, month, year or decade). This is the resolution (the commitment, the oath or the vow) which is expected to guide the affairs of the time manager over the identified period.

Although tasks have been set for him/her to accomplish, by his/her institution, he/she needs to be resolute on a number of tasks to be accomplished over different period of time on various aspects of his/her duties, as a scholar. He/she should always have one or more important things to accomplish for next year, next month, next week or next day.

It would be nice to hear the scholar in the rank of Senior Lecture saying that he/she has resolved to publish at least seven articles in some relevant indexed journals next year or to hear a ranked professor saying that in the next 5 years he/she would want to publish articles and books to earn more points than the points on publications that took him/her to the rank of professorship.

What about resolution on committed teaching, mentoring, guidance and counseling of undergraduate and graduate students? How nice would it be to Master's and PhD degrees supervisees if they hear that their supervisors have resolutions on producing reasonable numbers of students every year? As a community activist, the scholar should have some reasonable resolutions for the benefit of his/her immediate community, the working community and the larger community, depending on his/her position in each of the communities.

Setting a task for one self, all the times, makes a person him/her to be more focused and more result-oriented in his/her life. The scholar should be a leading example on this golden guide for effective time management.

10.20 Make Actions List and Cross off Tasks When Done

Mentally or in a note book, all activities planned for the day, week, month or year should be listed for treatment, one after another. The moment an activity is done with, the time manager should tick it on the list, continuously up to the end of the day, week, month or year. As an activity lined up is accomplished and ticked out, it makes the time manager to feel fulfilled, at least on that particular responsibility. What if one is able to take care of all the planned activities, within the limited time?

After drafting time budget, the scholar should list out all the important activities that must be accomplished in the course of achieving set objectives of the budget. For a day, one has to identify activities involving self and work place. These activities could be captured 'up-head' or they are put down in writing, somewhere for remembrance.

Usual daily time audit would show how good or bad was the day based on the important activities accomplished or not accomplished. The scholar should record at least 80% success on the accomplishment of the daily, weekly, monthly or yearly activities lined up for execution!

CHAPTER ELEVEN

RECAPITULATION AND RESEARCH POTENTIALS

11.1 Life of the Scholar

The life of the scholar is the soul of humanity, and that life has to be run successfully for humanity to record any tangible progress from generation to generation. The responsibilities to be discharged by the serious scholar are so numerous that effective time management must be adopted to accomplish those responsibilities within the limited time available.

For success in the life of the scholar, who is expected to always demonstrate academic and professional excellence, time must be effectively managed and utilised. This is the subject of emphasis in **Chapter One** of this book. It is hypothesised that successful scholars and other responsibility holders are always "good time managers"!

The Chapter also discusses the need for the scholar to master how to effectively manage his/her time and guide others on the best practice of time management. The fact that time is equally endowed on people generally was also discussed in the Chapter, arguing that the success of scholars and other users of time is, to a great extent, dependent on how they make good use of their endowed time.

Research Potentials: The absence of scientific proof on the argument that effective utilisation of time is a great determining factor to the success of a person in whatever he/she does for a living, suggests that there is a need for committed research on this issue to clear the air. If researches are to be conducted on this issue in various sectors and sub-sectors of various economies, the results would amount to a lot of contributions to knowledge in the field of time management.

11.2 Time Management Literature

The place of time management and its various aspects in the literature constitute the subjects of discussion in **Chapter Two.** A lot of "disappointing gaps" were discovered in the management science literature on knowledge production in respect of time management.

First it is clear that most of the efforts to popularise the field of time management were made by motivational speakers, consultants and coaches who wrote essays mainly in popular books or post onto their websites. Most of them conduct workshops, seminars or write coaching papers to guide mainly managers or directors of private and public sector organisations on the best way to manage their time, at a fee.

English-language-based scholarly works on time management and many aspects of it (skills, behaviors, attitudes, assessment/evaluation, etc) are scanty. Conceptual, theoretical and empirical papers in the area of time management published in indexed academic journals are few. This suggests that time management as a discipline is not enjoying the attention it deserves from researchers, especially those in the field of management science (business management/administration, accounting, finance, entrepreneurship, etc).

Due to the lackluster performance of management science scholars in the area of time management, there is the absence of universally acceptable definition of the concept of time management and other related terminologies like time, time planning, time wasters, time management skills, good time management behaviors, etc. Again, there is no clear theoretical framework for time management from the literature. All this calls for huge investment to be made by relevant academic institutions and professional bodies to embark on serious research and conferencing in this important area of study.

The Chapter also reveals some works done on time management from some religious perspectives, mainly Islamic and Christian points of views. Writers on time management from the perspectives of the two dominant religions in the world are in agreement that time management is about using time to worship God, to take care of the home front and to take care of the means of livelihood. Any other activity besides these three should not be given much attention as the limited endowed time is utilised.

Research Potentials: Conceptual, theoretical and empirical researches are needed on various aspects of time management that are not reasonably taken care of in the current literature. The results of these researches should be brainstormed at some international conferences/seminars so that consensus could be reached about the

96

concepts to be applied to various aspects of time management like time, time management, time management behaviors, time management skills, evaluation of its effectiveness, etc. These researches and conferences/seminars/congresses should also assist in developing universally acceptable theoretical framework for time management.

11.3 Concept of a Scholar

In **Chapter Three**, effort has been made to conceptualise a scholar, who is the focal point of analysis in the book. A scholar is described as a person who is sincerely committed to knowledge production activities in an academic institution. Some characteristics of a serious scholar are highlighted and discussed in the Chapter, including commitment to scholarship, sincerity of purpose, showing concern for future generation and working in an academic institution, like university, college, school, research institute/centre, etc.

The three main functions of the scholar: research, teaching and community service were discussed to show what must be done on each of the three before the person is respected as a serious scholar. It is concluded that a good scholar is student and servant of knowledge until the end of his/her life.

Research Potentials: Researches are needed on the time management behaviors of scholars working in different educational institutions, like research institutes/centers, universities, polytechnics, colleges, schools (basic and higher), or their equivalent. Do the scholars' behaviors in different institutions differ in their time management practices? Are the scholars in universities, for example, better time managers than the scholars in polytechnics or colleges of education? Are the time management practices of female scholars different from those of male scholars? What is the extent of the variation and why? What about the differences in the time management practices of young scholars and senior scholars? Are their differences between the time management practices of scholars working with educational institutions in developed economies and those working with educational institutions in developing economies? Is yes, what are the causes of the differences? These researches would assist in building up the time management literature very strongly and in developing a more scientific framework of effective time management in the life of the scholar.

11.4 Time Management Context

In the absence of universally acceptable definition of time management efforts, like the current book, have to be made to articulate some working definitions based on various perception of the concepts of time, time management, etc, pending the time consensus is reached (may be through seminars, conferences, conventions, etc) on how the concepts are to be universally defined. In **Chapter Four** of this book, some definitions are attempted in the context of the concern of the book, which is about the need for the scholar to always show effectiveness in time management.

Using some descriptions given to the term 'time' by the advanced learner's dictionary of current English in the 1998 and 2010 editions, the Chapter defines time as the indicator of the situation in the past, the present and the future, and that time could be defined in terms of second, minute, hour, day, week, month, year, decade, generation or century. On time management, the functions of management were used to accommodate time which is expected to be well managed and, so, it is defined as: the process of time planning, organising, directing and controlling by any time conscious user.

The Chapter also discusses how the scholar should be seen as a good time planner, organiser, controller, director and decision maker anywhere he/she find him-or herself. It is concluded that adherence to the functions of management (planning, organising, directing and controlling) to ensure effective time management and utilisation by scholars will go a long way in improving the quality of their decisions as academic leaders and chief administrators of the their research communities.

Research Potentials: There is need to find how scholars in various institutions actually plan the usage of their time, how they organise themselves within the limited time available, how they ensure good direction of their time, how they control the utilisation of their time, and the various decisions they take in the course of utilising their time. Comparative studies could be undertaken on scholars based on age groups, gender, locations, nature of institutions, etc. These studies are bound to "comb up" global best practices for all scholars to emulate/adopt.

11.5 Concern about Scarcity of Time

Scholars and other users of time complain a lot about scarcity of time, especially when they are not able to accomplish an important task within the given time. Chapter Five discusses the basic reason why time is scarce to its users generally and to scholars specifically. The reason is just that while the time available for a scholar to utilise is limited, the activities for him/her to perform are always unlimited.

Five other reasons why time appears to be always scarce to scholars and other users were discussed in the Chapter. The Chapter emphasises on the need for the scholar to effectively deal with scarcity of time, using different approaches suggested therein. An important strategy of dealing with scarcity of time is effective delegation to competent subordinates (if available). With the advent of technology, a serious scholar should not allow his/her work to be negatively affected by the apparent scarcity of time; he/she should always look for a way out so as to ensure that tasks are accomplished within the scarce time!

Research Potentials: There is need for researches to find out how scholars actually deal with time scarcity; how do some of them achieve much with the limited time available to them while others achieve less or none given the same quantity of time. If scholars in some educational institutions are found to be more productive academically than others working in other institutions that are located somewhere, should the better performance be linked to their ability to deal with time scarcity? While only six causes were suggested for time scarcity in this Chapter, a well designed empirical research work could discover ten or more causes of time scarcity among scholars, administrators, politicians, the military, CEOs, market women, postgraduate/undergraduate students, etc. Various strategies for dealing with the identified causes of time scarcity are bound to be discovered.

11.6 Conduct of Time Audit

Personal time audit is an independent examination of the way a time manager utilises his/her time during a particular point in time. It is conducted to ensure that the limited time is judiciously spent by the endowee; that the user knows actually where the time went, when and how. This is needed if time saving for more productive work in the future is the concern of the user.

Chapter Six discusses how personal time audit is to be conducted by the scholar daily, weekly and monthly, with a view to critically evaluate how he/she spends time and how time savings could be made in the future day, week, month or year. The time saved is to be effectively utilised by the scholar to take care of additional important tasks.

The Chapter shows that seven activities are in the forefront on competing for the limited time of the scholar: sleeping, personal life, work travels, leisure travel, domestic responsibilities, office responsibilities and having leisure. As time is allocated to these key activities, reasonableness principle should be exercised. An eight-itemed self-assessment questionnaire has been proposed to assist a scholar in exercising greater control over him-or herself and over all his/her activities.

Research Potentials: Do scholars actually conduct time audit? What are the difficulties of conducting the audit and, if they conduct, what are the benefits derived from the audit? These are research questions that need empirical answers. Moving forward, researches on the same subject matter could be conducted on the practice of time audit among supervisors, managers, directors or chief executives in the public, private and NGO (Non-Governmental Organisations) sectors of an economy. It would also be interesting to read about empirical research reports on the activities that actually consume scholar's time (seven were described in the Chapter), politician's time, CEOs' time, bankers' time, etc. Researches could also be conducted on how different categories of time managers rationalise the usage of their time, based on their peculiarities or the peculiarities of their organisations.

11.7 Who steals Scholars' Time?

Time stealers deny one the opportunity to make very good use of his/her time in accomplishing important tasks; they cause the limited time to get lost leaving the owner a sort of empty-handed! The scholar confronts time stealers every day, and care must be taken to ensure that they do not succeed in stealing away any share of his/her limited time.

Chapter Seven discusses five of the most dangerous time wasters to a scholar, including poor or absence of meeting objectives, telephone interruptions, lack of priority, the inability to finish assignment, and lack of self- discipline. Their causes and suggested solutions were highlighted to guide scholars and other time users on how to notice them and deal with them for personal effectiveness.

Research Potentials: There is the need to find out whether or not the time stealers discussed in this Chapter actually steal scholars' time and to what extent. What are other time stealers to scholars and how do they actually steal the scholars' time? Who faces the problem of time stealers more among young/new and old scholars; male and female scholars; scholars in developed economies and those in under-developed economies, scholars in universities and those in other research institutes; scholars in tertiary educational institutions and those at the high and basic schools levels? Studies could also be conducted on the negative effects of time stealers in other public and private sector organisations in different countries of the world.

11.8 General Time Wasting Behaviors of Scholars

Apart from the negative effects of time stealers on the productivity of scholars, whose causes and solutions have been highlighted in Chapter Seven, there are a number of times wasting behaviors many scholars exhibit. These general behaviors are discussed using some self-assessment questions/statements scholars are expected to give sincere responses to. Fourteen time wasting behaviors are presented in a statement form, demanding a simple 'yes' or 'no' answer to test whether the scholar is a time waster or not. A 'yes' respond suggests that the scholar is a time waster, while a 'no' response suggests that he/she does not exhibit time wasting behavior.

According to **Chapter Eight**, it is advisable that the scholar should just spend some few minutes to sincerely respond to the statements under each of the identified time wasters, with a simple 'Yes" or "No" answer. The scholar is to respond to the statements to self and not to any other examiner.

Research Potentials: It would be interesting to read reports of empirical researches on the effects of various time wasting behaviors of different categories of scholars, as well as those of other time users operating in different industries of different economies of the world. There is the need for management science scholars to find lasting scientific solutions to the problems of time wasting behaviors many users are suffering from.

11.9 Time Management Grid

Stephen R. Covey's time management grid/matrix is discussed in **Chapter Nine,** highlighting the four quadrants into which Covey categorises the various activities people conduct. The chapter emphasises the two key issues covered in the grid/matrix: importance and urgency. It is clear from the chapter that any activity that is not important or urgent should not be allocated any reasonable time. Also, activities that are both important and urgent should get the "lion share" of everybody's time.

Just as Covey insists that Quadrants 1 and 2 activities are to be taken care of before Quadrants 3 and 4 activities, Chapter 9 proposes that time allocation of scholars should be 50%: 30%: 15%: 05% for Quadrants 1, 2, 3 and 4 activities, respectively. Based on the peculiarities of the scholars at various levels and in different situations, appropriate adjustments could be made to this formula.

Research Potentials: Do scholars actually identify important and urgent activities for prioritisation in time allocation? How are scholars treating the activities categorised into the four Quadrants, and what has been their performance as a result? Which quadrant is enjoying the highest share of the scholars' time and which is getting the least share? These are some of the issues to be subjected to serious researches on the time management skills of scholars of various ranks, ages, gender, locations, etc. The issues could also be addressed in respect of government functionaries and public sector employees, private sector managers and employees, students at all levels, etc.

11.10 Golden Guide to Effective Time Management

What could be taken as the summary of all the important issues discussed to guide the scholars to be very effective and efficient time managers are enumerated and discussed in **Chapter Ten**. Twenty time management skills are "comb up" from the previous chapters' contents, especially the literature review conducted and reported in Chapter 2, to show that a scholar could actually make effective time management as a part of his/her life. The scholar is also expected to demonstrate that effective time management is actually a milestone to learning as a lifestyle.

Research Potentials: Each of the twenty (20) golden guides to time management demands an empirical research work to find out about its practicability in the life of the scholar and other responsibility holders, its implementation problems and solutions in all sectors of an economy, the likely benefits of implementing it to the time manager, to his/her organisation and to the economy as a whole.

BIBLIOGRAPHY

Abdullah, A. M. (1996). *Principles of Management and Leadership in Islam*, Riyadh: Al-Humaidhi Press (in Arabic).

Adair, J. (2000). *Effective Time Management*, UK: Pan MacMillan

Adams, G. A., & Jex, S. M. (1997). Confirmatory Factor Analysis of the Time Management Behavior Scale, *Psychological Reports*, 80(1), 225-226.

Adams, G. A., & Jex, S. M. (1999). Relationships between time management, control, work family conflict, and strain, *Journal of Occupational Health Psychology*, 4 (1), 72-77.

Adizes, I. (1989). *Corporate Life Cycles: How and Why Corporations Grow and Die and What to Do about It*, New Jersey: Englewood Cliffs

Afful-Broni, A. (2005). *Time management workshop for tertiary students. Winneba*: Faculty of Educational Studies. University of Education, Winneba. Unpublished Lecture Notes.

Afful-Broni, A. (2008). *Principles and practice of time management.* Accra, Ghana: Yamens Press Ltd.

Afful-Broni, A. (2013). Time Management Behavior among Academic and Administrative Staff of the University of Education, Winneba, *Journal of Education and Curriculum Development Research (JECDR)*, 1(3), 67-78

Alay, S. & Koçak, S. (2002). Validity and reliability of time management questionnaire. *Review of Faculty of Education*, *22*, 9-13.

Alexander, L. (1985). Successfully Implementing Strategic Decision, in *Long Range Planning*, 18 (3), 23-29

Al-Jeraisy, A. K. (2002). *Time Management From Islamic and Administrative Perspective*, Riyadh: Al-Jeraisy establishment.

Al-Jeraisy, K. (2001). *Time Management: An Islamic View*, Riyadh: International Islamic Publishing House, King Fahd National Library

Allen, D. (2001). *Getting things done: the art of stress free productivity*, New York: Penguin Books.

Allen, D. (2003). *Ready for anything: 52 productivity principles for work and life*, New York: Viking Books.

Anand, V. (2007). A study of time management: The correlation between video game usage and academic performance markers, *CyberPsychology & Behavior, 10* (4), 552-559.

Ancona, D. G., Goodman, P. S., Lawrence, B. S. & Tushman, M. L. (2001). Time: a new research lens, *Academy of Management Review*, 26, 645-663.

Anderson, L. W. (1984). An introduction to time and school learning, in Lorin, W. A. (Ed.) *Time and school learning*, London: Croon & Hill, 1-12.

Andrews, A. L. (2011). *Tell your time: how to manage your schedule so you can live free*. Chicago, IL: Amy Lynn Andrews.

Arnold, E., & Pulich, M. (2004). Improving productivity through more effective time management, *The Health Care Manager*, *23*(3), 65-70.

Ashkenas, R. N. & Schaffer, R. H. (1985). Managers can avoid wasting time., in *Winning the race against time: How successful executives get more done in a day*, Boston, MA: Harvard Business Review, 16-22.

Atkinson, D. (2001). The time crunch, *American Fitness, 19* (3), 37.

Azar, S. (2013). Impact of Time Management Training on Pakistani Corporate Sector Employees, *Journal of Basic and Applied Scientific research*. 3(4), 476-482

Azar, S. & Zafer, S. (2013). Confirmatory Factor Analysis of Time Management Behavior Scale: Evidence from Pakistan, *Interdisciplinary Journal of Contemporary Research in Business*, 4 (12), 946-959

Baiasu, S. (2011). Space, time and mind-dependence, *Kantian Review, 16(22)*, 175-190

Barkas, J. L. (1984). *Become more productive and still have fun: Creative time management*. Englewood Cliffs, New Jersey: Prentice-Hall, Inc.

Barling, J., Kelloway, E.K. & Cheung, D. (1996). Time management and achievement striving interact to predict car sale performance, *Journal of Applied Psychology*, 81, 821-826.

Bittman, M, Brown, J & Wajcman, J. (2009). The Cell Phone, Constant Connection and Time Scarcity in Australia, *Social Indicators Research*, 93(1), 229-233.

Blanchard, K. H. & Johnson, S. (1981). *The One Minute Manager*, La Jolla, CA: Blanchard- Johnson Publishers.

Blanchard, K. H. & Johnson, S. (1982). *The One Minute Manager*, New York: William Morrow & Co. 2nd Edition

Bliss, E. C. (1976). *Getting things done: The ABC's of time management*. New York: Charles Scribner's Sons.

Bond, M. Feather, N. (1988), "Some correlates of structure and purpose in the use of time", Journal of Personality and Social Psychology, Vol. 55, pp. 321-9.

Bond, M. J. & Feather, N. T. (1988). Some Correlates of Structure and Purpose in the Use of Time, *Journal of Personality and Social Psychology*, 55(2), 321-329.

Bond, M. J., & Feather, N. T. (1988). Some correlates and purpose in the use of time. *Journal of Personality and Social Psychology, 55*, 321-329.

Bregman, P. (2011). *18 minutes: find your focus, master distraction, and get the right things done.* New York: Grand Central Publishing.

Britton, B. & Tesser, A. (1991). Effects of time-management practices on college grades, *Journal of Educational Psychology*, 83, 405-410.

Britton, B. K. & Glynn, S. M. (1989). Mental Management and Creativity: A Cognitive Model of Time Management for Intellectual Productivity, in J. A. Glover, Chang, A. & Nguyen, L. T. (2011). The mediating effects of time structure on the relationships between time management behaviour, job satisfaction, and psychological well-being. *Australian Journal of Psychology*, 63(4), 187-197.

Brott, R. (2008). *Successful Time Management: Be The Productive Person*, London: ABC Book Publishing

Brown, K., Bradley, L., Lingard, H., Townsend, K. & Ling, S. (2010). Working Time Arrangements and Recreation: Making Time for Weekends when Working Long Hours, *Australian Bulletin of Labour*, 36(2), 194-213.

Burka, J. B., & Yuen, L. M. (1983). *Procrastination: Why you do it, what to do about it.* Reading, MA: Addison-Wesley.

Burke, M. A. (2001). *Time management. Bristol*, PA: The Falmer Press

Burnam, M. A., Pennebaker, J. W., & Glass, D. C. (1975). Time consciousness, achievement striving, and the Type A coronary prone behavior pattern. *Journal of Abnormal Psychology, 84*, 76-79.

Burt, C. D., & Kemp, S. (1994). Construction of activity duration and time management potential. *Applied Cognitive Psychology, 8*, 155-168.

Calabresi, R., & Cohen, J. (1968). Personality and time attitudes. *Journal of Abnormal Psychology, 73*, 431-439.

Canfield, A. A. (1976). *Time Perception Inventory.* Los Angeles, CA: Western Psychological Services.

Canfield, A. A. (1981). *Time Use Analyser.* Los Angeles, CA: Western Psychological Services.

Carlson, J. V. (2001). Review of Time Use Analyser, in B. S. Plake & J. C. Impara (Eds.), *The Fourteenth Mental Measurements Yearbook* Lincoln, NE: Buros Institute of Mental Measurements, 1276-1277.

Carrison, D. (2003). *Deadline! How premier organisations win the race against time*. Boston, MA: Amazon Kindle Books.

Cemaloglu, N. & Filiz, S. (2010). The Relationship between Time Management Skills and Academic Achievement of Potential Teachers, *Educational Research Quarterly, 33*(4), 3-23.

Chandler, S. (2011). *Time warrior: how to defeat procrastination, people-pleasing, self-doubt, over-commitment, broken promises and chaos*. Anna Maria, FL: Maurice Bassett.

Chapman, S. W. & Rupured, M. (2008). *Ten Strategies for Better Time Management,* the University of Georgia Cooperative Extension, May

Chua, W.F. (1986). Radical developments in accounting thought, *The Accounting Review*, Vol. 61(4), 601-32.

Claessens, B. J. C., Eerde, W. V., Rutte, C. G. & Roe, R. A. (2007). A Review of the Time Management Literature, *Personnel Review, 36* (2), 255-276.

Claessens, B.J.C., Van Eerde, W., Rutte, C.G. & Roe, R.A. (2004). Planning behavior and perceived control of time at work, *Journal of Organisational Behavior*, 25, 937-50.

Clegg, B. (1999). *Instant Time Management,* London: Kogan Page Publishers

Collins, C. (1987). *Time Management for Teachers: Practical Techniques and Skills That Give You More Time to Teach*. New York: Parker Press.

Conte, J. M., Mathieu, J. E. & Landy, F. J. (1998). The Nomological and Predictive Validity of Time Urgency, *Journal of Organisational Behavior*, 19, 1-13.

Conway, N. & Briner, R. B. (2002). A Daily Diary Study of Affective Responses to Psychological Contract Breach and Exceeded Promises, *Journal of Organisational Behaviour*, 23, 287-302.

Cooper, C. (2000). Choose Life, *People Management*, 11, 35-38.

Cooper, C. L., Sloan, S. J., & Williams, S. (1988). *Occupational Stress Indicator,* England: NFER Nelson.

Corwin, V., Lawrence, T. B., & Frost, P. J. (2001). Five strategies of successful part- time work. *Harvard Business Review, 79,* 121-127.

Covey, S. R. (1990). *The Seven Habits of Highly Effective People: powerful lessons in personal change.* New York: Simon and Schuster, Inc.

Covey, S. R., Merrill, A. R., & Merrill, R. R. (1994). *First Things First: To Live, to Love, to Learn, to Leave a Legacy.* New York: Simon & Schuster.

Cuny, J. (1999). Time Management and Family Issues, *Workshop paper presented to Women Academic,* University of Oregon, New Zealand

108

Dale, T. (1991). *Time Management*, Riyadh: Institute of Public Administration (in Arabic)

Dandago, K.I. (1998). *Time Management and Performance Improvement*, Paper presented to personnel officers in Kano State Primary Education Board (SPEB), at the Board Headquarters, Kano-Nigeria.

Dandago, K.I. (2000). *Time Management and Organisational Performance*, Paper presented to the staff of the National Women Centre, Abuja, Federal Capital Territory, Abuja, Nigeria

Dandago, K.I. (2002). *Time Management and Enhancement of Managers' Performance*, Paper presented to senior staff of Cement Company of Northern Nigeria (CCNN) Sokoto, premises of CCNN, Sokoto-Nigeria.

Dandago, K. I. (2003). *Auditing in Nigeria: A comprehensive Text*, Kano: Adamu Joji Publishers

Dandago, K.I. (2012). *Time Management for University Lecturer: A Milestone for Academic Excellence*, Paper presented to the new academic staff of Bayero University Kano, Nigeria, as part of the Orientation programme organised by Center for Continuing Education and Professional Development (CCEPD) Wednesday, 11th July.

Dandago, K.I. (2014). *Time Management in the Life of a Scholar: The Milestone to learning as a lifestyle*, Paper presented at the School of Accountancy, College of Business, Universiti Utara Malaysia (UUM) Public Lecture Series, 8th January

Davis, M. A. (2000). Time and the Nursing Home Assistant: Relations among Time Management, Perceived Control Over time, and Work-related Outcomes, Paper presented at the Academy of Management, Toronto, Canada.

DiPipi-Hoy, C., Jitendra, A. K., & Kern, L. (2009). Effects of time management instruction on adolescents' ability to self-manage time in a vocational setting. *The Journal of Special Education, 43*(3), 145-159.

Dishon-Berkovits, M. & Koslowsky, M. (2002). Determinants of employee punctuality, *The Journal of Social Psychology*, 142 (6), 723-739.

Dixon, M. S. (1993). Time Management: An essential Skill for the Successful Lawyer, *American Bar Association's Lawyering Skills Bulliten*, Vol 3 (2), 1-2

Dodd, P., & Sundheim, D. (2005). *The 25 Best Time Management Tools and Techniques: How to Get More Done Without Driving Yourself Crazy*. Ann Arbor, MI: Peak Performance Press, Inc.

109

Drawbaugh, C. C. (1984). *Time and its use: A Self-management guide for teachers.* NY: Teachers College Press.

Drucker, P. F. (1967). *The Effective Executive,* New York: Harper and Row.

Druker, P.F. (1964), *Managing for Results: Economic Tasks and Risk Taking Decisions,* Ahmedabad: Allied Publishers Ltd.

Edwards, J. (nd). The Importance of Time Management in the Christian Life, Internet Posting, www.biblicalchristianworldwide.net

Fahd, S. S. (1988). *Time Management: A developing Approach to Success,* Amman: Arab organisation for Administrative Sciences (in Arabic)

Farmer, S. & Seers, A. (2004). Time enough to work: employee motivation and entrainment in the workplace, *Time & Society,* 13, 265-84.

Feather, N. T., & Bond, M. J. (1983). Time structure and purposeful activity among employed and unemployed university graduates. *Journal of Occupational Psychology, 56,* 241-254.

Ferris, T (2007). *The 4-hour Workweek: Escape 9 – 5, Live Anywhere, and Join the New Rich.* Toronto: Crown Publishers/ Random House

Fitzgerald, M. & Waldrip, A. (2004a). Not enough time in the day: Media specialists, program planning, and time management, part 1. *Library Media Connection, August/September,* 38-40.

Fitzgerald, M. & Waldrip, A. (2004b). Still not enough time in the day: Media specialists, program planning, and time management, part 2. *Library Media Connection, October,* 26-28.

Flashman, R. H., Fetsch, R J. & Bradley, L A. (2008). The Successful Person's Guide to Time Management, *UK Cooperative Extension Service,* University of Kentucky

Foster, M. (2006). *Do it tomorrow and other secrets of time management.* Chicago, IL: P.H. Wyder.

Foust, J. (2000). Dewey Need to be Organised? Time management and Organisation from a Librarian Who knows Whereof She Speaks! *Book Report, 19* (2), 20.

Forsyth, P. (2013). *Successful Time Management,* 3rd Edition, London: Kogan Page Limited

Fox, M. L. and Dwyer, D. J. (1996). Stressful job demands and worker health: an investigation of the effects of self-monitoring, *Journal of Applied Social Psychology,* 25, 1973-1995.

Francis-Smythe, J. A., & Robertson, I. T. (1999). On the relationship between time management and time estimation. *British Journal of Psychology, 90,* 333-347.

Francis-Smythe, J. A. & Robertson, I. T. (1999). Time-related individual differences, *Time & Society*, 8, 273-92.

Frederick, S., Loewenstein, G. & O'Donoghue, T. (2002). Time discounting and time preference: A critical review, *Journal of Economic Literature*, 40 (2), 351-401.

Gafarian, C. T., Heiby, E. M., Blair, P., & Singer, F. (1999). The Diabetes time management questionnaire. *The Diabetes Educator*, 25, 585-592.

Gan Kong G., R, Kiong, P, Koh L. K., J. & Wong C., S. (2002). The impact of the Internet on the managers' working life, *Singapore Management Review*, 24 (2), 77-96.

Garba, A. M. (2001), *The Essence of Management*, Kano: Corporate Solutions Ltd.

Garcia-Ros, R., Pérez-González, F. & Hinojosa, E. (2004). Assessing Time Management Skills as an Important Aspect of Student Learning. *School Psychology International, 25*(2), 167-183.

Garhammer, M. (2002). Pace of Life and Enjoyment of Life, *Journal of Happiness Studies*, 3, 217-256.

George, J. M. & Jones, G. R. (2000). The role of time in Theory and Theory Building, *Journal of Management*, 26 (4), 657-684.

Gerdes, E. (2001). Managing time in a liberal education. *Liberal Education, 87* (2), 52-57.

Green, P. & Skinner, D. (2005). Does Time Management Training Work? An Evaluation, *International Journal of Training & Development*, 9(2), 124-139.

Griffiths, R.F. (2003). Time Management in Telework and Other Autonomous Work Environments, *Dissertation Abstract International: Section B: The Sciences and Engineering*, 64, 5B.

Hall, B. L. and Hursch, D. E. (1982). An Evaluation of the Effects of a Time Management Training Program on Work Efficacy, *Journal of Organisational Behaviour Management*, 3, 73-98.

Haneghan, J. P. (1995). Review of Checklist of Adaptive Living Skills, in Conoley, J. C. & Impara, J. C. (Eds.), *The Twelfth Mental Measurements Yearbook*, Lincoln, NE: Buros Institute of *Mental* Measurements, 171-175.

Harris, G. (1999). Redeeming the Time: A Christian Perspective on Time Management, Home Schooling, Internet Posting, www.biblicalchristianworldwide.net

Harris, J. (2008). *Time Management 100 Success Secrets*, Google Link: Lules. Com

Harvard Business School (2005). *Time management: Harvard Business Essentials.* Boston, MA: Harvard Business School Press

Hassan, H. A. (1995). *Skills of Time Management,* Cairo: The Centre for Enhancing Performance and Development (in Arabic)

Heller, R. (1995). *The Leadership Imperative,* Oxford: Heinemann press, England.

Hellsten, L. M. (2005). *The Development and Validation of a Time Management Scale for Exercise Adoption, Participation, and Adherence,* Doctoral thesis, University of Alberta, Canada, Archived by: Kinesiology Publications, University of Oregon, www.intechopen.com

Hellsten, L.M. & Rogers, W. T. (2009*)*. Development and preliminary validation of the Time Management for Exercise Scale, *Measurement in Physical Education and Exercise Science, 13,* 13-33.

Hellsten, L. M. (2012). What Do We Know About Time Management? A Review of the Literature and a Psychometric Critique of Assessment Instruments, in Stoilov, T. (Ed) *Time Management,* ISBN: 978-953-51-0335-6, InTech, 23rd March, Available from: http://www.intechopen.com/books/timemanagement/

Hendrickson, E. (2005). *The Tyranny of the To-do List. Chicago,* IL: Sticky Minds.

Hessing, M. (1994). More than clockwork: Women's time management in their combined workloads. *Sociological Perspective, 37(4),* 611-633.

Ho, B. (2003). Time management of final year undergraduate English projects: Supervisees' and the supervisor's coping strategies. *System, 31,* 231-245.

Hoch, D. (2000). Practical time-management for the AD, *Coach and Athletic Director, 70,* 12-13.

Hodgkinson, D. M. (1980). If I Only Had Time, *The Canadian Manager,* 5 (4), 14-18.

Hornby, A.S. (1998). *Oxford Advanced Learners Dictionary,* Oxford: Oxford University Press. P740.

Hornby, A.S. (2012). *Oxford Advanced Learners Dictionary,* Oxford: Oxford University Press. P762.

Jabnoun, N. (2001). Time Efficiency, a Chapter in *Islam and Management,* Riyadh: International Islamic Publishing House, King Fahd National Library, 52-55

Jackson, P. R. & Martin, R. (1996). Impact of just-in-time on job content, employee attitudes and well-being: a longitudinal study, *Ergonomics,* 39 (1), 1-16.

112

Jex, J. M. & Elacqua, T. C. (1999). Time management as a moderator of relations between stressors and employee strain, *Work and Stress*, 13, 182-191.

Jibreel, A. S. (1977). *Time: More Precious Than All Treasures on Earth*, Riyadh: Dar Ibn-Khuzaimah (in Arabic)

Jorde, P. (1982). *Avoiding burnout: Strategies for managing time, space, and people in early childhood education*. Washington, D.C.: Acropolis Books Ltd.

Kaufman, C. J., Lane, P. M. & Lindquist, J. D. (1991). Time congruity in the organisation: a proposed quality of life framework, Journal of Business and Psychology, 6, 79-106.

Kaufman-Scarborough, C. & Lindquist, J. D. (1999).Time management and polychronicity: comparisons, contrasts, and insights for the workplace, *Journal of Managerial Psychology*, 14, 288-312.

Kearns, H. & Gardiner, M. (2007). Is it time well spent? The relationship between time management behaviours, perceived effectiveness and work-related morale and distress in a university context, *Higher Education Research and Development*, 26 (2), 235-247.

Kelly, W. E. (2002). Harnessing the river of time: a theoretical framework of time use efficiency with suggestions for counselors, *Journal of Employment Counseling*, 39, 12-21.

Kelly, W. E. (2002). No time to worry: the relationship between worry, time structure, and time management. *Personality and Individual Differences, 35*, 1119-1126.

Kennedy, D. S. (2013). Time Management for Entrepreneur, 2nd Edition, NOBS: No S. S.

Khuldun, A. (1993). *Reflection on the Value of Time*, Beirut: Ad-Dar Ash-Shamiyyah (in   Arabic)

King, A., Winett, R. & Lovett, S. (1986). Enhancing coping behaviors in at-risk populations: the effects of time management instruction and social support in women from dual earner families, *Behaviour Therapy*, 17, 57-66.

Knight, B. (1989). *Managing school time*. Essex, Great Britain: Longman.

König, C. J. & Kleinmann, M. (2007). Time Management Problems and Discounted Utility, *The Journal of Psychology*, 141 (3), 321-334.

Kozoll, C. E. (1982). *Time management for educators*, Bloomington, Indiana: Phi Delta Kappa Educational Foundation.

Kuhl, J. & Fuhrmann, A. (1998). Decomposing self-regulation and self-control: the volitional components inventory", in Heckhausen, J. and

Dweck, C.S. (Eds), Motivation and Self-regulation Across The Life Span, Cambridge University Press, New York, NY, 15-49.

Lahmers, A. G. & Zulauf, C. R. (2000). Factors associated with academic time use and academic performance of college students: a recursive approach. *Journal of College Student Development*, 41, 544-556.

Lakein, A. (1973). *How to Get Control of your Time and Life*, New York: Nal Penguin Inc.

Landy, F. J., Rastegary, H., Thayer, J. & Colvin, C. (1991). Time Urgency: The Construct and Its Measurement. *Journal of Applied Psychology, 76*, 644-657.

Lang, D. (1992). Preventing short-term strain through time-management coping, Work & Stress, 6, 169-76.

Lang, R. J., Gilpen, J. L. & Gilpen, A. R. (1990). Stress-related symptoms among dental hygienists, *Psychological Reports, 66,* 715-722.

Lay, C. H. & Schouwenburg, H. C. (1993). Trait procrastination, time management and academic behaviour, *Journal of Social Behaviour and Personality*, 8, 647-662.

Leafe, G. H. (2004). Personal Time Management, Internet Posting, www.biblicalchristianworldwide.net

Macan, T. H. (1994). Time management: Test of a process model. *Journal of Applied Psychology, 79,* 381-391.

Macan, T. H. (1996). Time-management training: Effects on time behaviors, attitudes, and job performance, *The Journal of Psychology,* 130 (3), 229-236.

Macan, T. H., Shahani, C., Dipboye, R. L. & Phillips, A. P. (1990). College Students' Time Management: Correlations with Academic Performance and Stress, *Journal of Educational Psychology,* 82 (4), 760-768.

Mackenzie, R. A. (1972). *The time trap: How to get more done in less time.* New York: AMACOM.

Mackenzie, R. A. (1975). *New time management methods for you and your staff.* Chicago, IL: The Dartnell Corporation.

Mackenzie A (1997). *The time trap: the classic book on time management*, 3rd Edition, Boston, MA: The American Management Association.

Major, V. S., Klein, K. J. & Ehrhart, M. G. (2002). Work time, work interference with family, and psychological distress, *Journal of Applied Psychology*, 87, 427-36.

Major, V.S., Klein, K.J. & Ehrhart, M.G. (2002). Work time, work interference with family, and psychological distress, Journal of Applied Psychology, 87, 427-36.

Malone, S. & Jenster, P. (1991). Resting on Your Laurels: The Plateauing of the Owner-Manager, *European Management Journal,* 9 (4), 412-418.

Mancini, M. (2007). *Time Management: 24 Techniques to Make Each Minutes Count at Work,* Google Link: McGrow Hill

Marshall, J. C. (1998). *Proven Techniques for Making the Most of Your Valuable Time,* 1st edition New York: Bantam Press.

McCay, J. (1959). *The Management of Time,* New Jersey: Prentice Hallo, Englewood Cliffs.

McGrath, J. E., & Rotchford, N. L. (1983). Time and behavior in organisations, *Research in Organisational Behavior, 5,* 57-101.

McNamara, P. (2010). Factors influencing the time management behaviors of small business managers, *SBS HDR Student Conference, University of Wollongong* September 30), Paper 3, http://ro.uow.edu.au/sbshdr/2010/papers/3

Mingers, J. (2001). Embodying Information Systems: the Contribution of Phenomenology,
Information and Organisation, 11(2), 103 - 128

Mintzberg, H. (1973). *The Nature of Managerial Work,* New York: Harper and Row Ltd.

Misra, R., & McKean, M. (2000). College students' academic stress and its relation to their anxiety, time management, and leisure satisfaction. *American Journal of Health Studies, 16*(1), 41-51.

Mitchell, T. R. & James, L. R. (2001). Building better theory: time and the specification of when things happen, *Academy of Management Review,* 26, 530-47.

Mohamed, A. A. (1999). *More Precious Than Gold,* Riyadh: Dar Al-watan (in Arabic)

Mohamed, A. J. (1992). *Time: Construction or Destruction,* Kuwait: Dar Ad-Da'wah (in Arabic)

Morgenstein, J. (2004). *Time management from the inside out: the foolproof system for taking control of your schedule and your life.* New York: Bantam Press.

Morreau, L. E. & Bruininks, R. H. (1991). *Checklist of Adaptive Living Skills.* Itasca, IL: The Riverside Publishing Company.

Morris, T. (2001). *101 time smart solutions for teachers,* Winnipeg, MB: Portage & Main Press.

115

Mpofu, E., D'Amico, M. & Cleghorn, A. (1996). Time management practices in an African Culture: Correlates with College Academic Grades. *Canadian Journal of Behavioural Sciences, 28*(2), 102-112.

Mudrack, P. (1997). The structure of perceptions of time, Educational and Psychological Measurement, 57, 222-40.

Mudrack, P. (1997). The structure of perceptions of time, *Educational and Psychological Measurement*, 57, 222-40.

Muhammad U. S., Ehsan, N., Hameed, F., Khan, M. A. & Rahim, J. (2011). High Level Principles of Time Management in Islam, *International Conference on Sociality and Economics Development IPEDR* 10, 290-295

Nickel, J. (2003). Clock: The Heritage of the Christian Faith, *The Chelcedon Report*

Onacken, W. Jr. & Wass, D. L. (1985). Management time: Who's got the monkey? In *Winning the Race Against Time: How Successful Executives Get More Done in a Day*, Boston, MA: Harvard Business Review, 49-54.

Orlikowsky, W. J. & Yates, J. (2002). It's about time: Temporal structuring in organisations, *Organisation Science*, 13, 684-700.

Orpen, C. (1993). The effect of time-management training on employee attitudes and behavior: A field experiment. *The Journal of Psychology, 128 (4),* 393-396.

Osbourne, R. (1995). How to fit exercise into your day. *Current Health, 2* (1), 22-24.

Palmer, D. K. & Schoorman, F. (1999). Unpackaging the Multiple Aspects of Time in Polychronicity, *Journal of Managerial Psychology*, 14(3 & 4), 323-344.

Peach, D. (2012). Ten Tips on Time Management for the Busy Christian, Internet Posting, www.biblicalchristianworldwide.net

Peeters, M. A. G. & Rutte, C. G. (2005). Time-management behavior as a moderator for the job demand-control interaction, *Journal of Occupational Health Psychology*,10, 64–75.

Pentland, W.E., Harvey, A.S., Lawton, M.P. & McColl, M.A. (1999), *Time Use Research in the Social Sciences,* New York: Kluwer Academic/Plenum Publishers.

Perlow, L.A. (1999). The Time Famine: Towards a Sociology of Work Time, *Administrative Science Quarterly*, 44, 57-81.

Perry, J. A. (1997). First things first: Prioritising and time management. *Black Collegian, 28* (1), 54-60.

Puffer, S. M. (1989). Task-completion schedules: Determinants and consequences for performance. *Human Relations, 42,* 937-955.

Quarshie, T.V. (2002). Moving up the corporate Ladder: Useful Hints for Women Executives, in *Management in Nigeria,* the official Journal of NIM, 33(2), April –June, 4.

Randel, J. (2010). *The Skinny on Time Management: How to Maximize Your 24-Hour Gift,* Google Link: Rand Media Co.

Rau, R. & Triemer, A. (2004). Overtime in relation to blood pressure and mood during work, leisure, and night time, *Social Indicators Research,* 67, 51-73.

Reis, H.T. & Wheeler, L. (1991). Studying social interaction with the Rochester Interaction Record, *Advances in Social Psychology,* 24, 269-318.

Rice, H. C. (1984). Leadership: Part two, time management. *Scholastic Coach, 54*(4), 44, 46, 75.

Richards, J. H. (1987). Time management: A Review, *Work and Stress,* 1, 73-78.

Sabelis, I. (2001). Time management: paradoxes and patterns, *Time & Society,* 10, 387-400.

Schmidt, A. M. & DeShon, R. P. (2007). What to do? The effects of discrepancies, incentives, and time on dynamic goal prioritisation, *Journal of Applied Psychology,* 92(4), 928-941.

Schmidt, A. M., Dolis, C. M. & Tolli, A. P. (2009). A matter of time: Individual differences, contextual dynamics, and goal progress effects on multiple-goal self-regulation, *Journal of Applied Psychology,* 94 (3), 692-709.

Schriber, J. B., & Gutek, B. A. (1987). Some time dimensions of work: Measurement of an underlying aspect of organisation culture. *Journal of Applied Psychology, 72,* 642-650.

Schuler, R. S. (1979). Managing stress means managing time. *Personnel Journal, December,* 851-854.

Sean, M. (2010). Successful Time Management, *MTD Training,* London, UK: Ventus Publishing ApS

Shahani, C., Weiner, R. & Streit, M. K. (1993). An investigation of the dispositional nature of the time management construct, *Anxiety, Stress, and Coping,* 6, 231-43.

Shanti, D. G. (2009). *24-hour champion: discovering and living your priceless lif*e. Seattle, W.A: Create Space.

Shipman, N. (1983). *Effective time-management techniques for school administrators*, New Jersey: Prentice-Hall.

Simons, D. J. & Galotti, K. M. (1992). Everyday planning: An analysis of daily time management. *Bulletin of the Psychonomic Society, 30* (1), 61-64.

Simpson, B. G. (1978). Effective time management. *Parks & Recreation, 13* (9), 61-63.

Slaven, G. & Totterdell, P. (1993). Time management training: does it transfer to the workplace?, *Journal of Managerial Psychology*, 8, 20-8.

Smith, J. (1999). Life planning: Anticipating future life goals and managing personal development, *in* Brandtstädter, J. & Lerner, R. M. (Eds.), *Action & social development: Theory and research through the life span*, Thousand Oaks, CA: Sage. pp. 223-255.

Smith, S. (2002). Tolerating Uncertainty: The exploration of a 10-week stress management course which supports a process of recovery, personal change and educational development for people experiencing stress and anxiety. *Research in Post-Compulsory Education, 7,* 211-227.

Sonnentag, S. & Schmidt-Braße, U. (1998). Expertise at work: research perspectives and practical interventions for ensuring excellent performance at the workplace, *European Journal of Work and Organisational Psychology,* 7, 449-454.

Soucie, D. (1986). Proper Management of Your Time. *CAHPER Journal, 52* (2), 36.

Spinks, N. (2004). Work-Life Balance: Achievable Goal or Pipe Dream? *The Journal for Quality and Participation,* 27(3), 4-11.

Stanley, F. C. (2002). Success God's Way: True Contentment and Purpose, London: UK Thomas Nelson Publishers.

Stephen, H. (1988). *A Brief History of Time,* New York: Bantam Press.

Stevens, M. J. & Pfost, K. S. (1984). Stress Management Interventions. *Journal of College Student Personnel, May,* 269-270.

Strongman, K.T. & Burt, C. D. B. (2000). Taking breaks from work: an exploratory inquiry, *Journal of Psychology,* 134, 229-42.

Swart, A. J., Lombard, K. & De Jager, H. (2010). Exploring the Relationship between Time Management Skills and the Academic Achievement of African Engineering Students: A case study. *European Journal of Engineering Education, 35*(1), 79-89.

Sweidel, G. B. (1996). A project to enhance study skills and time management, *Teaching of Psychology,* 23, 246-8.

Taylor, J. & Mackenzie, R. A. (1986). Time is money, so use it productively. *ABA Banking Journal, April,* 130-131.

Teuchmann, K., Totterdell, P. & Parker, S.K. (1999). Rushed, unhappy, and drained: an experience sampling study of relations between time pressure, perceived control, mood, and emotional exhaustion in a group of accountants, *Journal of Occupational Health Psychology,* 4 (1), 37-54.

Tracy, B. (2007). *Time power: a proven system for getting more done in less time,* New Training House, Inc.

Trueman, M. & Hartley, J. (1995). Measuring Time Management Skills: a Cross-cultural Study. Paper Presented at the American Educational Research Association, San Francisco.

Trueman, M. & Hartley, J. (1996). A Comparison between the Time Management and Academic Performance of Mature and Traditional-entry University Students. *Higher Education, 32,* 199-245.

Van de Meer, J., Jansen, E., & Tarenbeek, M. (2010). It's Almost a Mindset that Teachers Need to Change: First-year Students' Need to be Inducted into Time Management. *Studies in Higher Education, 35*(7), 777-791.

Van Eerde, W. (2003). Procrastination at Work and Time Management Training, *Journal of Psychology,* 137, 421-34.

Vodanovich, S.J. & Seib, H. M. (1997). Relationship Between Time Structure and Procrastination, *Psychological Reports,* 80, 211-5.

Wachter, J. C., & Carhart, C. (2003). *Time-saving Tips for Teachers,* 2nd ed, Thousand Oaks, CA: Corwin Press.

Walsh, R. (1998). *Time Management: Proven Techniques for Making Every Minute Count,* 7th Edition Avon, MA: Adams Media

Warner, J. (2002). *Time Management Effectiveness Profile Facilitators,* UK: Human Resource Development Press

Waterhouse, J. & Colley, L. (2010). The Work-Life Provisions of the Fair Work Act: A Compromise of Stakeholder Preference, *Australian Bulletin of Labour,* 36(2), 154-177.

Weber, M., & Vogel, H. G. (1979). *Human Factor Structure Affecting Time Allocation Behavior Modification.* Paper presented at the Recreation and Park Administrators' Seminar, Seebe, Alberta.

Wessman, A. E. (1973). Personality and the Subjective Experience of Time, *Journal of Personality Assessment, 37* (2), 103-114.

White, A. (2001). Priorities: A Time Management Skill for PROHs to Learn. *Medical Teacher, 23,* 215-216.

Williams, R. L, Verble, J. S., Price, D. E. & Layne, B. H. (1995). Relationship between Time Management Practices and Personality Indices and Types, *Journal of Psychological Type, 34,* 36-42.

Winter, M., Puspitawati, H., Heck, R. K. & Stafford, K. (1993). Time Management Strategies Used by Households With Home-based Work, *Journal of Family and Economic Issues, 14*(1), 69-94.

Winwood, R. I. (1990). *Time Management: An Introduction to the System,* Franklin: Franklin International Institute

Woolfolk, A. E. & Woolfolk, R. L. (1986). Time Management: An Experimental Investigation, *Journal of School Psychology,* 24, 267-75.

Wratcher, M.A. & Jones, R.O. (1988). A Time Management Workshop for Adult Learners, *Journal of College Student Personnel,* 27, 566-567.

Wright, T.A. (2002). Dialogue: The Importance of Time in Organisational Research, *Academy of Management Journal,* 45, 343-345. www.biblicalchristianworldwide.net

Yoels, W. C. & Clair, J. M. (1994). Never Enough Time: How Medical Residents Manage a Scarce Resource, *Journal of Contemporary Ethnography, 23* (2), 185-213.

Yusuf, A. (1997). *Time in the Muslim's Life,* Beruit: Mua'ssat Arrisalah (in Arabic)

Zaheer, S., Albert, S. & Zaheer, A. (1999). Time Scales and Organisational Theory, *Academy of Management Review,* 24, 725-741.

Zemetakis, L. A., Bouranta, N. & Moustakis, V. S. (2010). On the Relationship Between Individual Creativity and Time Management, *Thinking Skills and Creativity, 5,* 23-32.

Zerihun, T. B. & Krishna, S. M. (2012). A Few Techniques of Time Management, *Journal of Businss Management and Social Science Research,* 1(3), 32-37

Zijlstra, F.R.H., Roe, R. A., Leonora, A. B. & Krediet, I. (1999). Temporal Factors in Mental Work: Effects of Interrupted Activities, *Journal of Occupational and Organisational Psychology,* 72, 163-185.

Zinatelli, M., Dube, M. A. & Jovanovic, R. (2002). Computer-based Study Skills Training: The Role of Technology in Improving Performance and Retention, *College Student Retention, 4* (1), 67-78.

OTHER BOOKS BY THE AUTHOR

Dandago, K. I., Dahiru, A. M. & Oseni, O. A. (eds) (2013). *Essentials of Islamic Banking and Finance in Nigeria,* Ibadan, Nigeria: Benchmark Publishing Company Limited

Dandago, K. I. & Kurawa, J. M. (eds) (2012). *Researches in Contemporary Accounting Issues,* Kano- Nigeria: Kamba Digital Printing and Publishing Company in conjunction with the Department of Accounting, Bayero University. (426 pages)

Dandago, K. I., Liman, M. M. & Ahmed, A. B.(eds) (2011). *Converting Kano State Resource-based Economy to Tax-based,* Kano-Nigeria: Published by Triumph Publishing Company in conjunction with the Faculty of Law, Bayero University, Kano- Nigeria. (250 pages)

Dandago, K. I. & Tijjani, B. (eds) (2011). *Corporate Governance and Social Responsibility,* Kano- Nigeria: Department of Accounting, Bayero University in conjunction with Adamu Joji Publishing Company Ltd. (390 pages)

Dandago, K. I., Baffa, A. U. & Adamu, Y. M.(eds) (2010). *Issues in Youth Development: A Multidisciplinary Perspective,* Kano- Nigeria: Adamu Joji Publishing Company Ltd. (414 pages)

Dandago, K. I. (ed) (2009). *Contemporary Issues in Accounting, Auditing and Taxation,* Kano- Nigeria: Department of Accounting, Bayero University in conjunction with the Triumph Publishing Company Ltd. (327 pages)

Dandago, K. I. and Muktar, M.(eds) (2009). *Quantitative Techniques in Social and Management Sciences,* Kano-Nigeria: Faculty of Social and Management Sciences, Bayero University, Kano- Nigeria in conjunction with Adamu Joji Publishing Company Ltd. (294 pages)

Dandago, K. I. & Obisasan, D. O. (2009). *Financial Reporting and Ethics,* Lagos: The Institute of Chartered Accountants of Nigeria (ICAN), (269 pages). Study Pack for ICAN and other Accounting Students.

Dandago, K. I. (ed) (2009). *Advanced Accounting Theory and Practice,* London: Adonis and Abbey Publishing Company Limited. (285 Pages)

Dandago, K. I. & Tahir, K. H. (eds)(2007). *Commitment and Due Process,* Proceedings of the 4th National Conference on Ethical Issues in Accounting, Department of Accounting, Bayero University, Kano, Nigeria, Vol. 4 (306 pages)

Dandago, K. I., Idris, M. & Muktar, M.(2007). *Mathematics for Social Sciences,* Kano- Nigeria: Faculty of Social and Management Sciences, Bayero

University, in conjunction with Adamu Joji Publishing Company Ltd. (107 pages)

Dandago, K. I., Adamu, Y.M. & Mohammed, H. (eds) (2006). *Readings in Social Science Research*, Kano, Nigeria: Faculty of Social and Management Sciences, Bayero University in conjunction with Adamu Joji Publishing Company Limited. (276 pages)

Dandago, K. I. & Atuilik, E.W. (2006). *Cost Accounting and Budget*, Lagos: The Association of Accountancy Bodies in West Africa (ABWA), (375 pages). Study Pack for ATSWA and other Accounting Students

Dandago, K. I. (2006), *Beyond Slogans: How States Hold the Ace for Nigeria's Industrialization*, Ibadan-Nigeria: Benchmark Publishing Company Ltd. (156 pages).

Dandago, K. I. & Tahir, K. H. (eds) (2005). *Honesty and Integrity*, Proceedings of the Third National Conference on Ethical Issues in Accounting, Department of Accounting, Bayero University, Kano, Nigeria, Vol. 3. (317 pages)

Dandago, K. I. & Koya, S.B. (2005). *Cost Accounting*, Lagos: The Institute of Chartered Accountants of Nigeria (ICAN) (362 pages). Study Pack for ICAN and other Accounting Students.

Dandago, K. I. & Tanko, A. I. (eds) (2004). *Prudence, Transparency and Accountability*, Proceedings of the Second National Conference on Ethical Issues in Accounting, Department of Accounting, Bayero University, Kano, Nigeria, Vol. 2 (473 pages).

Dandago, K. I. (ed)(2004). *Accounting and Internal Control Systems in Practice*, Kano, Nigeria: Department of Department of Accounting, Bayero University in conjunction with Adamu Joji Publishing Company Limited. (139 pages)

Dandago, K. I. (2004), *Financial Accounting Simplified*, 2nd Edition, Kano-Nigeria: Adamu Joji publishing company Ltd. (543 pages)

Dandago, K. I. & Tijjani, B. (2003). *Cost and Management Accounting*, Lagos: Malthouse Press Limited. (560 pages)

Dandago, K. I. & Tanko, A. I. (eds) (2003). *Background Issues to Ethics in Accounting*, Proceedings of the First National Conference on Ethical Issues in Accounting, Department of Accounting, Bayero University, Kano, Nigeria, Vol.1. (326 pages)

Dandago, K. I. (2003). *Straight Way to Success in Accounting (for Secondary School Students)*, 2nd edition, Kano-Nigeria: Adamu Joji publishing company Ltd. (245 pages)

122

Dandago, K. I. (2003). *Auditing in Nigeria: A Comprehensive Text*, 2nd edition, Kano- Nigeria: Adamu Joji publishing company Ltd. (261 pages)

Dandago, K. I. & Alabede, J. O. (2000). *Taxation and Tax Administration in Nigeria*, Kano-Nigeria: Triumph Publishing Company Ltd. (269 pages)

Dandago, K. I. (ed) (2000). *Management Information System: A Practical Emphasis*, Kano-Nigeria: Adamu Joji Publishing Company Ltd. (127 pages)

INDEX

H

habit · 24, *See* also Stephen R. Covey
humanity · 17, 33, 37, 38, 42, 43, 82, 83, 87, 95

J

job · 22, 26, 28, 32, 55, 66, 107, 110, 112, 114, 116, *See* also satisfaction

K

key · 15, 65, 77, 100, 102
knowledge · 31, 32, 37, 38, 39, 40, 42, 82, 86, 88, 95, 96, 97

L

leisure · 29, 31, 33, 56, 57, 58, 100, 115, 117
literature · 17, 19, 20, 23, 24, 25, 26, 27, 29, 30, 34, 38, 95, 96, 97, 102

M

management · 15, 16, 17, 19, 20, 21, 22, 23, 24, 25, 26, 27, 28, 29, 30, 31, 32, 33, 34, 42, 43, 44, 45, 46, 47, 51, 52, 58, 60, 65, 70, 77, 80, 81, 83, 84, 88, 89, 92, 96, 97, 98, 101, 102, 105, 106, 107, 110, 112, 113, 114, 115, 116, 117, 118, *See* also functions
matrix · 17, 77, 78, 83, 84, 102, *See* also time management
mentor · 41, 58, 68, *See* also coach
mentoring · 23, 46, 70, 94

O

objectives · 15, 16, 28, 32, 35, 43, 44, 45, 46, 54, 66, 70, 78, 83, 85, 86, 88, 94, 100
organising · 15, 23, 27, 28, 31, 43, 44, 45, 47, 60, 70, 76, 98

P

planning · 15, 21, 27, 28, 31, 32, 43, 44, 45, 47, 51, 70, 74, 76, 80, 81, 85, 88, 96, 98, 110, 118
poor · 16, 17, 21, 38, 50, 51, 55, 58, 65, 68, 69, 70, 72, 74, 75, 76, 83, 100, *See* also time management
priority · 33, 45, 65, 66, 71, 76, 79, 88, 100
professional · 15, 19, 20, 21, 22, 24, 25, 34, 38, 41, 45, 53, 55, 58, 78, 95, 96
programmes · 34, 58, *See* also zero
projects · 29, 79, 82, 112

Q

qual-quan · *See* also research

R

religion · 30, *See* also faith
research · 19, 24, 25, 26, 27, 34, 35, 37, 38, 39, 40, 42, 45, 47, 51, 52, 54, 57, 80, 81, 85, 87, 89, 95, 96, 97, 98, 99, 100, 101, 103, 106, 118
responsibilities · 15, 17, 28, 37, 40, 41, 42, 43, 45, 49, 54, 56, 57, 59, 65, 66, 69, 70, 71, 72, 74, 75, 76, 77, 78, 79, 80, 81, 82, 85, 90, 91, 92, 93, 95, 100
results · 27, 38, 40, 42, 46, 53, 67, 69, 84, 88, 90, 92, 95, 96

S

satisfaction · 22, 23, 26, 28, 29, 89, 107, 115, *See* also job
scarcity · 17, 25, 49, 50, 51, 52, 85, 99
scholar · 15, 17, 37, 38, 39, 40, 41, 42, 44, 45, 46, 47, 49, 50, 51, 52, 53, 54, 55, 56, 57, 58, 59, 60, 61, 63, 64, 65, 66, 67, 68, 69, 70, 71, 72, 73, 74, 75, 76, 77, 78, 79, 80, 81, 82, 83, 84, 85, 86, 87, 88, 89, 90, 91, 92, 93, 94, 95, 97, 98, 99, 100, 101, 102, 103
services · 22, 37, 41, 47, 50, 54, 57, 60
skills · 25, 26, 27, 29, 30, 34, 46, 59, 96, 97, 102, 118

125

T

V

W

Z

www.ingramcontent.com/pod-product-compliance
Lightning Source LLC
Chambersburg PA
CBHW070407200326
41518CB00011B/2104